D0807516

Dogs 101: A Guide to American Kennel Club Breed Groups, Vol. 5 - The Toy Group

Jacob Cleveland

Contents

Articles

References

Dog breed

Dog breeds are groups of closely related and visibly similar domestic dogs, which are all of the subspecies *Canis lupus familiaris*, having characteristic traits that are selected and maintained by humans, bred from a known foundation stock.

The term ***dog breed*** may also be used to refer to *natural breeds* or landraces, which arose through time in response to a particular environment which included humans, with little or no selective breeding by humans. Such breeds are undocumented, and are identified by their appearance and often by a style of working. Ancient dog breeds are some of the modern (documented) descendants of such *natural breeds*.

Dog breeds are not scientifically defined biological classifications, but rather are groupings defined by clubs of hobbyists called breed clubs.

A ***dog breed*** is represented by a sufficient number of individuals to stably transfer its specific characteristics over generations. Dogs of same breed have similar characteristics of appearance and behavior, primarily because they come from a select set of ancestors who had the same characteristics. Dogs of a specific breed breed true, producing young closely similar to the parents. An individual dog is identified as a member of a breed through proof of ancestry, using genetic analysis or written records of ancestry. Without such proof, identification of a specific breed is not reliable. Such records, called stud books, may be maintained by individuals, clubs, or other organizations.

Classification

In biology, subspecies, race and breed are equivalent terms. Breed is usually applied to domestic animals; species and subspecies, to wild animals and to plants; and race, to humans. Colloquial use of the term *dog breed*, however, does not conform to scientific standards of taxonomic classification. Breeds do not meet the criteria for subspecies since they are all considered a subspecies of the gray wolf; an interbreeding group of individuals who pass on characteristic traits and would likely merge back into a single homogeneous group if external barriers were removed. The recognition of distinct dog breeds is not maintained by a scientific organization; they are maintained by a number of independent kennel clubs that need not apply to scientific standards and are often inconsistent. For instance, the Belgian Shepherd Dog is separated into four distinct breeds by some clubs, but not in others. Further, some groups of dogs which clearly share a persistent set of characteristics and documented descent from a known foundation stock may still not be recognized by some clubs as breeds. For instance, the feist is a hunting dog raised in the Southern United States for hunting small game. Feists have a consistent set of characteristics that reliably differentiate them from other dog types and breeds. However, the United Kennel Club recognizes one breed of feist, the Treeing Feist, while the American Kennel Club does not recognize any feist breed.

A dog is said to be purebred if its parents were purebred and it meets the standards of the breed. Purebred dog breeders of today "have inherited a breeding paradigm that is, at the very least, a bit anachronistic in light of modern genetic knowledge, and that first arose out of a pretty blatant misinterpretation of Darwin and an enthusiasm for social theories that have long been discredited as scientifically insupportable and morally questionable." Morally questionable policies regarding purity of breed include obligatory surgical procedures to spay or neuter animals in numerous contexts. The American Kennel Club, for instance, allows mixed-breed dogs to be shown but requires these animals to be altered. It does not make such requirements for purebred dogs. California Assembly Act AB 1634 was a bill introduced in 2007 that would require all non-working dogs of mixed breed over the age of 6 months to be neutered or spayed. The bill was morally controversial, leading the American Kennel Club to fight the bill.

The clear genetic distinction between breeds of dog has made dogs of specific breeds good subjects for genetic and human medical research. "Using the dog as a discovery tool" in studying how cancer affects specific breeds may lead to identifying "susceptibility genes that have proved intractable in human families and populations."

History of dog breeds

Pariah dogs originally established themselves near human populations, developing and maintaining themselves without further selection. They do not carry any specialized working dog functions. Working, hunting and other functional breeds most likely appeared when there was a demand for certain traits and humans were able to devote time and resources to perfect those traits.

Initial dog selections centered on helpful behavior such as barking at unfamiliar creatures and people, guarding livestock, or hunting game. Some dog breeds, such as Saluki or New Guinea Singing Dogs , have been bred for thousands of years. Some working dog breeds such as German Shepherd or Labrador Retriever were established in the last few hundred years. More recently, dogs have been selected for attractiveness and distinctive features, resulting in a vast variety of different breeds. Similar dog breeds are classified by dog registries in Dog Breed Groups.

Groups of individuals that have dogs of the same breed often unite into national breed clubs, describing their dogs in specific language by writing a breed standard. Breed standards prescribe the most desirable specimen attributes and working abilities for purebred dogs of that breed as well as undesirable traits. National breed clubs promote their breeds via the local breed registry and international organizations. Dogs recognized by the main breed registries are said to be "purebred".

Development of dog breeds

For the history and development of the dog, see Origin of the domestic dog, Ancient dog breeds, and Dog type.

There is much speculation but little evidence about why canids came to live with or near humans, possibly as long as 100,000 years ago. With the beginnings of agriculture around 12,000 years ago, humans began making use of dogs in various ways, resulting in physical differences between dogs and their wolf ancestors. In earlier times, little was written about dogs, although there were known dog types or landrace dogs, which developed over time with minimal human intervention, to fit in with the environment (including human culture) in which the dogs lived or live. Dog breeds in the modern sense date only to the accurate documenting of pedigrees with the establishment of the English Kennel Club in 1873, in imitation of other stud book registries for cattle and horses.

Many dog breeds today have names of original landrace types, such as the Border Collie. Other landrace types, such as retrievers, have been made more uniform in appearance through selective breeding, and developed into a variety of distinctive breeds. Varieties of purebred dogs kept for working purposes can vary in appearance from purebred dogs of the same breed kept as showdogs and pets.

New dog breeds are being continually created. They are either accidentally or purposely crossbred from existing breeds, developed for a specific style of work, or created just for marketing purposes. Recently discovered semi-feral and landrace types such as the New Guinea Singing Dog have been documented and registered as breeds for purposes of preservation. The Canadian department of agriculture has strict standards for the documenting of what it calls "emerging breeds". Many registries which require minimal documentation are available for registering new and existing breeds of dog. In general, a dog can only be guaranteed to be of a specific breed if it is documented in the stud book of a major dog registry or breed registry.

Genetics

Dog breeds can now be analyzed through genetics. Genetic markers (microsatellite markers and single-nucleotide polymorphisms) have been analyzed and a representative sample of 85 breeds were placed into four clusters, each cluster having shared ancestors. Cluster 1 is thought to be the oldest, including African and Asian dogs. Cluster 2 is mastiff type dogs; cluster 3 is herding dogs, and cluster 4 modern hunting type dogs (mostly developed in Europe in the 1800s.)

- **Note: Relationships uncovered through genetics may not match "official" breed histories.** The following breed lists are based on genetic research, not traditional beliefs about dog breeds.

- Cluster 1 (Thought to be older lineages): Afghan Hound, Akita Inu, Alaskan Malamute, Basenji, Chow Chow, Irish Wolfhound, Lhasa Apso, Pekingese, Saluki, Samoyed, Shar Pei, Shiba Inu, Shih Tzu, Siberian Husky, Tibetan Terrier.

- Cluster 2 (Mastiff-type): Bernese Mountain Dog, Boxer, Bulldog, Bullmastiff, French Bulldog, German Shepherd Dog, Cierny Sery, Greater Swiss Mountain Dog, Labrador Retriever, Mastiff, Miniature Bull Terrier, Newfoundland, Pomeranian, Presa Canario, Rottweiler.

- Cluster 3 (Herding): Belgian Sheepdog, Belgian Tervuren, Borzoi, Collie, Greyhound, Pug, St. Bernard, Shetland Sheepdog.

- Cluster 4 (Modern/hunting dogs): Airedale Terrier, American Cocker Spaniel, American Hairless Terrier, American Water Spaniel, Australian Shepherd, Australian Terrier, Basset Hound, Beagle, Bedlington Terrier, Bichon Frise, Bloodhound, Border Collie, Cairn Terrier, Cavalier King Charles Spaniel, Chesapeake Bay Retriever, Chihuahua, Clumber Spaniel, Dachshund, Doberman Pinscher, English Cocker Spaniel, Flat Coated Retriever, German Shorthaired Pointer, Giant Schnauzer, Golden Retriever, Great Dane, Ibizan Hound, Irish Setter, Irish Terrier, Italian Greyhound, Keeshond, Kerry Blue Terrier, Komondor, Kuvasz, Manchester Terrier, Miniature Schnauzer, Norwegian Elkhound, Old English Sheepdog, Pharaoh Hound, Pointer, Portuguese Water Dog, Pit Bull Terrier, Rhodesian Ridgeback, Schipperke, Soft Coated Wheaten Terrier, Standard Poodle, Standard Schnauzer, Welsh Springer Spaniel, West Highland White Terrier, Whippet.

Dog breed documentation

Stud books

Dog breeds are documented in lists of antecedents called a stud book.

Dog breeds that have been documented may be accepted into one or more of the major registries (kennel clubs) of dog breeds, including the Fédération Cynologique Internationale (covering 84 countries), The Kennel Club (UK), the Canadian Kennel Club, the American Kennel Club, the United Kennel Clubs International, the Australian National Kennel Council and the New Zealand Kennel Club, and other national registries. The registry places the breed into the appropriate category, called a Group. Some Groups may be further subdivided by some registries. When the breed is fully accepted, the stud book is closed and only dogs bred from dogs in the stud book will be accepted for registration. These dogs are referred to as purebred.

Dog breed clubs, especially of dogs bred for a particular kind of work, may maintain an open stud book and so may not be included in major registries. The dogs are still considered a breed. An example of this would be the Jack Russell Terrier Club of America.

Some dog breeds fit the definition of breed, especially breeds that develop naturally on islands or in isolated areas, but are few in number or have not been sufficiently documented to be registered with one of the major registries. An example of this would be the Kintamani Dog and other rare or independent breeds.

Breeds of dogs can be deliberately created in a relatively short period of time. When they breed true and have been sufficiently documented, they can be accepted by major registries. An example of this is the Cesky Terrier.

Breed Standards

Each dog breed has a written Breed Standard, a list of attributes that standardises the appearance of the breed, written by the breed's founder or breed club. Dog are judged in Conformation Dog Shows on the basis of how closely the individual dog conforms to the breed standard. As the breed standard only covers external aspects of the dog's appearance, breeding working dogs for show competition may cause appearance to be emphasised to the detriment of working ability.

Groups of dogs mistaken for breeds

Groups of dogs that may be mistaken for breeds include working dogs that are categorized by working style rather than appearance, although they may be of various ancestry and may not breed true. The difference between a named group of working dogs and a breed of dogs can be unclear. Examples would be the huntaway and other livestock dogs of New Zealand, the feist dogs of the southern United States, and the Patagonian sheepdogs of Argentina, which are collies mixed with other working dogs.

Landrace dogs are another grouping that often have been named but are not always considered breeds. "Landrace" is a term used for early types domesticated animals, including dogs, where isolated populations of dogs are selected according to human goals; developing over time rather than through modern breeding techniques. An example of a landrace dog would be the dog described as 'Basset' as early as 1585. The landrace Basset was developed into the modern breeds of Dachshund and Basset Hound, as well as modern day terrier breeds.

Another group of dogs that may be mistaken for breeds are the progeny of intentional crossbreedings of two purebred dogs. These popularity of these crosses are often the result of fads. Examples include the Puggle and the Labradoodle.

Mixed breed dogs may be offered a form of registration to allow them to participate in organized dog events. Often given the name All-American or AMBOR dog, the name does not signify that dogs so registered are a breed. Dogs must be spayed or neutered to be registered.

Individual dogs or small groups of dogs may use an existing breed name or be given an invented breed name and listed with little or no documentation for a fee with "registry" companies with minimal verification requirements. The dogs are then bred and marketed as a "registered" breed, sometimes as a "rare" or new breed of dogs.

See also

General

- Ancient dog breeds
- List of dog breeds
- Breed Clubs
- List of most popular dog breeds
- Rare breeds

Health Issues

Dog health as it relates to dog breeds is well documented in the following articles:

- Conformation show
- Dog
- Dog health
- Dog breeding
- List of dog diseases
- Canine reproduction
- Inbreeding
- Animal testing
- Founder effect
- Health of a specific breed is covered in the article for that breed.

External links

- AKC Dog Registration Statistics for 2003 and 2004 [1]
- Fédération Cynologique Internationale, lists 339 dog breeds in 78 groups [2]
- Rare Breed Network, alphabetic list of new, rare, local, and numerically smaller breeds [3]
- Dog breed photos and facts [4]
- AKC Dog Registration Statistics for 2003 and 2004 [1]
- The Best Dogs for Pets [5] The best breeds dogs for pets
- From Canada's Guide to Dogs [6] - basic information about registered dog breeds and reputable all-breed registries as well as information about registries "not able to meet the more demanding requirements of the CKC (Canadian Kennel Club), AKC, or UKC."
- Just Dog Breeds [7]
- Diversity and the pure bred dog [8]
- CompareCanines.com - Compare 150+ dog breeds in over 50 different categories [9]
- Dog Breed Dictionary [10]
- Federacion Canina Internacional [11]

American Kennel Club

The **American Kennel Club** (or **AKC**) is a registry of purebred dog pedigrees in the United States. Beyond maintaining its pedigree registry, this kennel club also promotes and sanctions events for purebred dogs, including the Westminster Kennel Club Dog Show, an annual event which predates the official forming of the AKC, the National Dog Show, and the AKC/Eukanuba National Championship. Unlike most other country's kennels clubs, the AKC is not part of the Fédération Cynologique Internationale (World Canine Organization).

Dog registration

The AKC is not the only registry of purebred dogs, but it is the only non-profit registry and the one with which most Americans are familiar. Founded in 1884, the AKC is the largest purebred dog registry in the world. Along with its nearly 5,000 licensed and member clubs and affiliated organizations, the AKC advocates for the purebred dog as a family companion, advances canine health and well-being, works to protect the rights of all dog owners and promotes responsible dog ownership. An example of dogs registered elsewhere in the U.S. is the National Greyhound Association which registers racing greyhounds (which are legally not considered "pets").

For a purebred dog to be registered with the AKC, the dog's parents must be registered with the AKC as the same breed, and the litter in which the dog is born must be registered with the AKC. If the dog's parents are not registered with the AKC or the litter is not registered, special registry research by the AKC is necessary for the AKC to determine if the dog is eligible for AKC registration. Once a determination of eligibility is met, either by litter application or registry research, the dog can be registered as purebred by the AKC.To register a mixed breed dog with AKC as a Canine Partner, you may go to the AKC website and enroll the dog via an online form. Once registered, your mixed breed dog will be eligible to compete in the AKC Agility, Obedience and AKC Rally® Events. 2010 Most Popular Dogs in the U.S.

1. Labrador Retriever

2. German Shepherd Dog

3. Yorkshire Terrier

4. Golden Retriever

5. Beagle

6. Boxer

7. Bulldog

8. Dachshund

9. Poodle

10. Shih Tzu

Registration indicates only that the dog's parents were registered as one recognized breed; it does not necessarily indicate that the dog comes from healthy or show-quality blood lines. Nor is registration necessarily a reflection on the quality of the breeder or how the puppy was raised. Registration is necessary only for breeders (so they can sell registered puppies) or for purebred conformation show or purebred dog sports participation. Registration can be obtained by mail or online at their website.

AKC and health

Even though the AKC supports some canine health research and has run advertising campaigns implying that the AKC is committed to healthy dogs, the AKC's role in furthering dog health is controversial. Temple Grandin maintains that the AKC's standards only regulate physical appearance, not emotional or behavioral health. The AKC has no health standards for breeding. The only breeding restriction is age (a dog can be no younger than 8 months.) Furthermore, the AKC prohibits clubs from imposing stricter regulations, that is, an AKC breed club cannot require a higher breeding age, hip dysplasia ratings, genetic tests for inheritable diseases, or any other restrictions. Parent clubs do have the power to define the looks of the breed, or breed standard. Parent club may also restrict participation in non-regular events or classes such as Futurities or Maturities to only those dogs meeting their defined criteria. This enables those non-regular events to require health testing, DNA sampling, instinct/ability testing and other outlined requirements as established by the hosting club of the non-regular event.

As a result, attention to health among breeders is purely voluntary. By contrast, many dog clubs outside the US do require health tests of breeding dogs. The German Shepherd Club of Germany [1], for example, requires hip and elbow X-rays in addition to other tests before a dog can be bred. Such breeding restrictions are not allowed in AKC member clubs. As a result, some US breeders have established parallel registries or health databases outside of the AKC; for example, the Berner Garde [2] established such a database in 1995 after genetic diseases reduced the average lifespan of a Bernese Mountain Dog to 7 years. The Swiss Bernese Mountain Dog club introduced mandatory hip X-rays in 1971.

For these, and other reasons, a small number of breed clubs have not yet joined the AKC so they can maintain stringent health standards, but, in general, the breeders' desire to show their dogs at AKC shows such as the Westminster Dog Show has won out over these concerns.

Contrary to most western nations organized under the International Kennel Federation (of which the AKC is not a member), the AKC has not removed docked tails and cropped ears from the requirements of many AKC breed standards, even though this practice is opposed in the U.S. by the American Veterinary Medical Association, and banned by law in many other countries.

The Club has also been criticized for courting large scale commercial breeders.

Purebred Alternative Listing Program / Indefinite Listing Privilege Program

The Purebred Alternative Listing Program (PAL), formerly the Indefinite Listing Privilege Program (ILP), is an AKC program that provides purebred dogs who may not have been eligible for registration a chance to register "alternatively" (formerly "indefinitely"). There are various reasons why a purebred dog might not be eligible for registration; for example, the dog may be the product of an unregisterable litter, or have unregisterable parents. Many dogs enrolled in the PAL and ILP programs were adopted from animal shelters or rescue groups, in which case the status of the dog's parents is unknown. Dogs enrolled in PAL/ILP may participate in AKC companion and performance activities, but not conformation. Enrollees of the program receive various benefits, including a subscription to *Family Dog* Magazine, a certificate for their dog's place in the PAL, and information about AKC Pet Healthcare and microchipping. Dogs that were registered under the ILP program keep their original numbers.

AKC National Championship

The AKC/Eukanuba National Championship is an annual event held in both Tampa, FL, and Long Beach, CA. The show is by invitation only. The dogs invited to the show have either finished their championship from the bred-by-exhibitor class or ranked in the Top 25 of their breed. The show can often be seen on major television stations.

Open foundation stock

The Foundation Stock Service (FSS) is an AKC program for breeds not yet accepted by the AKC for full recognition, and not yet in the AKC's Miscellaneous class. The AKC FSS requires that at least the parents of the registered animal are known. The AKC will not grant championship points to dogs in these breeds until the stud book is closed and the breed is granted full recognition.

Activities

The AKC sanctions events in which dogs and handlers can compete. These are divided into three areas:

- Conformation shows
  - Junior Showmanship
- Companion events, in which all registered and PAL/ILP dogs can compete. These include:
  - Obedience trials
  - Tracking trials
  - Dog agility
  - Rally obedience

- Performance events, which are limited to certain entrants; PAL/ILP dogs of the correct breed are usually eligible:
  - Coonhound events (coonhounds; no PAL/ILP dogs)
  - Field trials (hounds)
  - Earthdog trials (small terriers and Dachshunds)
  - Sheepdog trials (herding tests) (herding breeds, Rottweilers, and Samoyeds)
  - Hunt tests (most dogs in the Sporting Groups and Standard Poodles)
  - Lure coursing (sighthounds only)
  - Working Dog Sport (obedience, tracking, protection) German Shepherds, Doberman Pinschers, Rottweilers, Bouvier des Flandres

AKC policy toward working dog sport events that include protection phases, such as Schutzhund, has changed according to prevailing public sentiment in the United States. In 1990, as well-publicized dog attacks were driving public fear against many breeds, the AKC issued a ban on protection sports for all of its member clubs. After the terrorist attacks of 9/11/2001, Americans began to take a more positive attitude toward well-trained protection dogs, and in July 2003 the AKC decided to allow member clubs to hold a limited number of protection events with prior written permission. In 2006 the AKC released rules for its own Working Dog Sport events, very similar to Schutzhund.

In 2007, the American Kennel Club accepted an invitation from the Mexican Kennel Club to participate in the Fédération Cynologique Internationale World Dog Show in Mexico City.

Recognized breeds

As of July 2009, the AKC fully recognizes 163 breeds with 12 additional breeds granted partial status in the Miscellaneous class. Another 62 rare breeds can be registered in its Foundation Stock Service.

The AKC divides dog breeds into seven *groups*, one *class*, and the Foundation Stock Service, consisting of the following (as of July 2009):

- Sporting Group: 28 breeds developed as bird dogs. Includes Pointers, Retrievers, Setters, and Spaniels.
- Hound Group: 25 breeds developed to hunt using sight (sighthounds) or scent (scent hounds). Includes Greyhounds and Beagles.
- Working Group: 26 large breeds developed for a variety of jobs, including guarding property, guarding livestock, or pulling carts. Includes Siberian Huskies and Bernese Mountain Dogs.
- Terrier Group: 27 feisty breeds some of which were developed to hunt vermin and to dig them from their burrows or lairs. Size ranges from the tiny Cairn Terrier to the large Airedale Terrier.
- Toy Group: 21 small companion breeds Includes Toy Poodles and Pekineses.

- Non-Sporting Group: 17 breeds that do not fit into any of the preceding categories, usually larger than Toy dogs. Includes Bichon Frises and Miniature Poodles.

- Herding Group: 22 breeds developed to herd livestock. Includes Rough Collies and Belgian Shepherds.

- Best in Show:over 150 breeds All Breeds

- Miscellaneous Class: 11 breeds that have advanced from FSS but that are not yet fully recognized. After a period of time that ensures that good breeding practices are in effect and that the gene pool for the breed is ample, the breed is moved to one of the seven preceding groups.

- Foundation Stock Service (FSS) Program: 62 breeds. This is a breed registry in which breeders of rare breeds can record the birth and parentage of a breed that they are trying to establish in the United States; these dogs provide the *foundation stock* from which eventually a fully recognized breed might result. These breeds cannot participate in AKC events until at least 150 individual dogs are registered; thereafter, competition in various events is then provisional.

The AKC Board of Directors appointed a committee in October, 2007, to evaluate the current alignment of breeds within the seven variety groups. Reasons for the action included the growing number of breeds in certain groups, and the make-up of breeds within certain groups. The number of groups and group make-up has been modified in the past, providing precedent for this action. The Group Realignment Committee completed their report in July, 2008.

The committee recommended that the seven variety groups be replaced with ten variety groups. If this proposal is approved, the Hound Group would be divided into "Scent Hounds" and "Sight Hounds"; the Sporting Group would be divided into "Sporting Group – Pointers and Setters" and "Sporting Group – Retrievers and Spaniels"; a new group called the "Northern Group" would be created; and the Non-Sporting Group would be renamed the "Companion Group". The Northern Group would be populated by Northern/Spitz breeds, consisting of the Norwegian Elkhound, Akita, Alaskan Malamute, Siberian Husky, Samoyed, American Eskimo, Chinese Shar-Pei, Chow Chow, Finnish Spitz, Keeshond, Schipperke, Shiba Inu and Swedish Vallhund. In addition, the Italian Greyhound is proposed to be moved to the Sight Hound Group, and the Dalmatian is proposed to be moved to the Working Group.

See also: American Kennel Club Groups

Other AKC programs

The AKC also offers the Canine Good Citizen program. This program tests dogs of any breed (including mixed breed) or type, registered or not, for basic behavior and temperament suitable for appearing in public and living at home.

The AKC also supports Canine Health with the Canine Health Foundation http://www.akcchf.org/

Another AKC affiliate is AKC Companion Animal Recovery (AKC CAR), the nation's largest not-for-profit pet identification and 24/7 recovery service provider. AKC CAR is a leading distributor of pet microchips in the U.S. and a participant in AAHA's free Pet Microchip Lookup tool.

AKC and legislation

The AKC tracks all dog related legislation in the United States, lobbies lawmakers and issues legislative alerts on the internet asking for citizens to contact public officials. They are particularly active in combating breed-specific legislation such as bans on certain breeds considered dangerous. They also combat most legislation to protect animals such as breed-limit restrictions and anti-puppy mill legislation. While they argue that their motive is to protect legitimate breeders and the industry, many argue their incentive is purely financial.

See also

- List of dog breeds
- United Kennel Club
- DOGNY
- American Dog Club
- World Wide Kennel Club
- List of Kennel Clubs by Country

External links

- Official website [3]
- AKC CAR's Official website [4]
- 2007 Registration Data [1]
- The Politics of Dogs: Criticism of Policies of AKC [5] The Atlantic, 1990
- Digging into the AKC: Taking cash for tainted dogs [6] The Philadelphia Inquirer, 1995
- Doogle.Info Worldwide online dog database and pedigree [7]

Toy Group

Toy Group is the name of a breed Group of the smallest kinds of dogs, used by kennel clubs to classify a defined collection of dog breeds. *Toy Group* does not necessarily refer to one particular type of dog. Most major English-language kennel clubs include a *Toy Group* although different kennel clubs may not include the same breeds in their *Toy Group*. The international kennel club association, the Fédération Cynologique Internationale, includes toy dogs in Group 9 *Companion and Toy Dogs*, which is then further broken down into eleven *Sections* based on dog type and breed history.

Toy dogs

The use of the term *toy* to refer to dogs is based on tradition, and is not a precise classification. Dogs traditionally referred to as *toy dogs* are usually the very smallest dogs. *Toy dogs* can be one of several dog types. Some are of ancient lap dog types, and some are small versions of hunting dog, Spitz, or terrier types, bred down in size for a particular kind of work or to create a pet of convenient size. The very smallest dogs are sometimes called *Teacup*, although no major dog registry recognizes that term.

The term "toydog" is also criticized, as pets should not be considered being toys. Although there has been attempts to change the term to another, more fitting, there has been no luck.

Toy Group breeds

In general, kennel clubs assign small breeds that are primarily kept as companions and pets to their *Toy Group*. Some kennel clubs prefer to use the category Companion Group for small and medium-sized dogs kept primarily as pets, and do not recognise a *Toy Group*. Other kennel clubs group small dogs with large dogs of the same type, or in the Utility Group or Non-Sporting Group.

Comparison of Toy Group breeds of major kennel clubs

Toy Group breeds of major kennel clubs

The Kennel Club (UK) Toy Group	Canadian Kennel Club Toy Dogs Group	American Kennel Club Toy Group	Australian National Kennel Council Toy Dogs Group	New Zealand Kennel Club Toy Group
Affenpinscher	Affenpinscher	Affenpinscher	Affenpinscher	Affenpinscher
Australian Silky Terrier	Cavalier King Charles Spaniel	Brussels Griffon (elsewhere Griffon Bruxellois)	Australian Silky Terrier	Australian Silky Terrier
Bichon Frise	Chihuahua (Long Coat)	Cavalier King Charles Spaniel	Bichon Frise	Bichon Frise

Bolognese	Chihuahua (Short Coat)	Chihuahua (one breed)	Cavalier King Charles Spaniel	Bolognese
Cavalier King Charles Spaniel	Chinese Crested	Chinese Crested	Chihuahua (Long Coat)	Cavalier King Charles Spaniel
Chihuahua (Long Coat)	Coton de Tulear	English Toy Spaniel (elsewhere King Charles Spaniel)	Chihuahua (Smooth Coat)	Chihuahua (Long Coat)
Chihuahua (Smooth Coat)	English Toy Spaniel (elsewhere King Charles Spaniel)	Havanese	Chinese Crested Dog	Chihuahua (Smooth Coat)
Chinese Crested	Griffon (Brussels) (elsewhere Griffon Bruxellois)	Italian Greyhound	English Toy Terrier (Black & Tan)	Chinese Crested Dog
Coton De Tulear	Havanese	Japanese Chin	Griffon Bruxellois	English Toy Terrier (Blk & Tan)
English Toy Terrier (Black and Tan)	Italian Greyhound	Maltese	Havanese	Griffon Bruxellois
Griffon Bruxellois	Japanese Spaniel (elsewhere Japanese Chin)	Toy Manchester Terrier	Italian Greyhound	Havanese
Havanese	Maltese	Miniature Pinscher	Japanese Chin	Italian Greyhound
Italian Greyhound	Miniature Pinscher	Papillon	King Charles Spaniel	Japanese Chin
Japanese Chin	Papillon	Pekingese	Lowchen (Little Lion Dog)	King Charles Spaniel
King Charles Spaniel	Pekingese	Pomeranian	Maltese	Lowchen
Lowchen (Little Lion Dog)	Pomeranian	Poodle (Toy only)	Miniature Pinscher	Maltese
Maltese	Poodle (Toy)	Pug	Papillon	Miniature Pinscher
Miniature Pinscher	Pug	Shih Tzu	Pekingese	Papillon
Papillon	Silky Terrier (elsewhere Australian Silky Terrier)	Silky Terrier (elsewhere Australian Silky Terrier)	Pomeranian	Pekingese
Pekingese	Toy Manchester Terrier	Toy Fox Terrier	Pug	Pomeranian
Pomeranian	Yorkshire Terrier	Yorkshire Terrier	Tibetan Spaniel	Pug
Pug	Xoloitzcuintli (Toy)		Yorkshire Terrier	Yorkshire Terrier
Yorkshire Terrier				

Fédération Cynologique Internationale Group 9 Sections

The Fédération Cynologique Internationale breaks down their Toy and Companion Group into *Sections* by general dog type; within the sections the dogs are listed by their country or area of origin. Also included in the Sections are variants and colours that have to do with how they are organised during dog shows. Since this grouping is for more than Toy dogs, not all of the dogs included in Group 9 are small.

The sections are:

- *Section 1: Bichons and related breeds*

Maltese	Bichon Frise	Havanese
Bolognese	Coton de Tuléar	Löwchen

- *Section 2: Poodle*

Poodle (Toy)

- *Section 3: Small Belgian Dogs*

Belgian Griffon	Griffon Bruxellois (*Brussels Griffon*)	Petit Brabancon

- *Section 4: Hairless Dogs*

Chinese Crested

- *Section 5: Tibetan breeds*

Lhasa Apso	Shih Tzu	Tibetan Spaniel
Tibetan Terrier		

- *Section 6: Chihuahueño*

Chihuahua (Smooth-haired)	Chihuahua (Long-haired)

- *Section 7: English Toy Spaniels*

Cavalier King Charles Spaniel	King Charles Spaniel (*English Toy Spaniel*)

- *Section 8: Japan Chin and Pekingese*

Pekingese	Japanese Chin

- *Section 9: Continental Toy Spaniel*

Papillon (with erect ears)   Phalène (with drooping ears)

- ### *Section 10: Kromfohrländer*

Kromfohrlander

- ### *Section 11: Small Molossian type Dogs*

French Bulldog   Pug   Boston Terrier

The remainder of breeds assigned to the *Toy Group* by other kennel clubs are placed with larger dog breeds of the same type by the Fédération Cynologique International; for example, the toy size terriers are in *Group 3, Section 2, Small-sized terriers* or *Group 3, Section 4, Toy Terriers.*

Not included in the Fédération Cynologique Internationale *Group 9, Companion and Toy* are these breeds that are listed in the *Toy Group* of some kennel clubs:

- Terrier-type breeds included in the *Toy Group* of some kennel clubs:

Australian Silky Terrier   English Toy Terrier (Black & Tan)   Manchester Terrier

Toy Fox Terrier   Yorkshire Terrier

- Spitz-type dogs included in the *Toy Group* of some kennel clubs:

Pomeranian   Schipperke

- Pinscher-type dogs included in the *Toy Group* of some kennel clubs:

Affenpinscher   Miniature Pinscher

- Sighthound-type dogs included in the *Toy Group* of some kennel clubs:

Italian Greyhound

Other clubs

The United Kennel Club (US) is often considered among the major kennel clubs; it does not recognise a *Toy Group* (see Companion Group for a comparison.)

Most clubs in non-English speaking countries also list small dogs in either a *Toy Group* or a *Companion Group.*

Very small dogs are also included in the listings of the enormous and ever-expanding number of specialty registries, minor kennel clubs, dog sports clubs, breed clubs, rare dog registries, and internet based dog clubs and businesses. Each will have its own definition of what breeds belong in their own

Toy Group.

In addition, Toy dogs in particular have been used for crossbreeding to create what are called designer dogs, bred either accidentally or to enhance the marketability of puppies, often with cute portmanteau names created from syllables of each breed name. Although there are clubs willing to "register" such designer dogs, they are not breeds of dog. They may be called *toy dogs* but they are not part of any *Toy Dog Group*.

See also

- Breed Groups (dog)
- Toy dog
- Pet
- Lap dog
- Companion dog
- Companion Group

Affenpinscher

The **affenpinscher** is a terrier-like toy breed of dog.

Description

Appearance

Weighing 7 to 9 pounds (3-4 kg) and not exceeding 11 inches (24-30 cm) in height at the withers, the affenpinscher has harsh rough coat and a monkey-like expression (*Affe* means monkey in German). Its coat is shaggier over the head and shoulders forming a mane, with shorter coat over the back and hind quarters. It is harsh and wiry in texture. The FCI and UK breed standards specifies that the coat must be black, but the AKC also allows gray, silver, red,and tan, and belge (not beige; belge is a mixture of red, black and white hairs); other clubs have their own lists of acceptable colours, with black being the preference. The affenpinscher is a dog with a shaggy, wiry-type coat.

Temperament

Affenpinschers have a distinct appearance that some associate with terriers. They are different from terriers, however, in that they are actually part of the pinscher-schnauzer of group 2 in the FCI classification and so often get along with other dogs and pets. They are active, adventurous, curious, and stubborn, but they are also fun-loving and playful. The breed is confident, lively, affectionate towards family members and is also very protective of them. This loyal little dog enjoys being with its family. It needs consistent, firm training because some can be quite difficult to housebreak. The training should be varied because the dog can easily become bored. The affenpinscher has a terrier like personality.

Affenpinschers are somewhat territorial when it comes to their toys and food, so they are not recommended for very small children. This dog is mostly quiet but can become very excited if attacked or threatened and shows no fear toward any aggressor. It is best suited for a family who likes a show and has a sense of humor.

Health

Mortality

A small sample (N=21) of affenpinschers in a UK survey had a median lifespan of 11.4 years, which is a typical lifespan for a purebred dog, but a bit lower than most breeds of their size. The most common causes of death were old age (24%), urologic (19%), and "combinations" (14%)..Some are prone to fractures, slipped stifle, pda, open fontanel and respiratory problems in hot weather.

Morbidity

The affenpinscher is prone to hip dysplasia. As with many small breeds of dog they are prone to collapsed trachea, which is best avoided by walking the dog with a harness instead of a collar. Cataracts are occasionally reported.

History

The breed is German in origin and dates back to the seventeenth century. Its name is derived from the German *Affe* (ape, monkey). The breed predates and is ancestral to the Griffon Bruxellois (Brussels Griffon) and Miniature Schnauzer.

Dogs of the Affenpinscher type have been known since about 1600 but these were somewhat larger, about 12 to 13 inches, and came in colors of gray, fawn, black and tan, gray and tan, and also red. White feet and chest were also common. The breed was created to be a ratter, working to remove rodents from kitchens, granaries, and stables.

Care

Affenpinschers need to be groomed two to three times a week.

Shedding

Affenpinschers often appears on lists of dogs that allegedly do not shed (moult). However, every hair shaft in the dog coat grows from a hair follicle. Each shaft has a cycle of growing, then dying and being replaced by another shaft. When the hair shaft dies, the hair is shed. The length of time of the growing and shedding cycle varies by breed, age, and by whether the dog is an inside or outside dog. "There is no such thing as a nonshedding breed."

Frequent grooming reduces the amount of loose fur in the environment.

See also

- Companion Dog Group
- Companion dog
- Toy Group
- Griffon Bruxellois
- dog

External links

Clubs, associations and societies

- Affenpinscher Club of America [1]
- The Affenpinscher Club (UK) [2]
- Affenpinscher Rescue [3]

Informational Websites

- American Kennel Club - Affenpinscher [4]
- Affen World [5]

Griffon Bruxellois

The **Griffon Bruxellois** or **Brussels Griffon** is a breed of toy dog, named for their city of origin: Brussels, Belgium. The Griffon Bruxellois may refer to three different breeds, the **Griffon Bruxellois**, the **Griffon Belge** and the **Petit Brabançon**. Identical in standard except for coat and colour differences, in some standards they are considered varieties of the same breed, much like Belgian Sheepdogs.

Description

Temperament

The Griffon Bruxellois is known to have a huge heart, and a strong desire to snuggle and be with his or her master. They display a visible air of self-importance. A Griffon should not be shy or aggressive; however, they are very emotionally sensitive, and because of this, should be socialized carefully at a young age. Griffons should also be alert, inquisitive and interested in their surroundings.

Griffons tend to bond with one human more than others. This, along with their small size, may make them unsuitable as a family pet, especially for a family with very small children. Griffons tend to get along well with other animals in the house, including cats, ferrets, and other dogs. However, they can get into trouble because they have no concept of their own relative size and may attempt to dominate dogs much larger than themselves.

Some say: "Having a Griffon means having a true constant companion. They need their favorite person all the time, and will be very unhappy if left outdoors or alone most of the day. A Griffon Bruxellois will want to follow you about the house, on your errands, and to bed."

Health

Compared with many other breeds, Griffons have few inherited health issues.. It is thought that these few health problems have long existed in the breed, and only in recent years these issues have been identified and categorized. The typical life span of a Griffon is somewhere in the range of 12 to 15 years.

Birthing

Griffons usually have no trouble whelping on their own, but sometimes complications can cause a caesarean section to be needed. The size of a litter is typically 1-3 puppies. The size of the litter often determines the extent of these complications. It is not unheard of for a litter to have six in it. When they are born, the puppies only weigh but a few ounces and are small enough to fit in the palm of an adult's hand.

Cleft palate

One issue that is typically fatal for the puppies is having a cleft palate. It results in the puppy not receiving nourishment from the mother and eventually starvation. It is uncommon but, depending on the size of the cleft it is possible for the puppy to survive where as it becomes older surgery can be done to close the hole.

Eyes

- **Lacerations** - Lacerations are a common issue amongst the breed. Because the Griffons have such large eyes and a short snout, there is very little there to protect their vision from foreign bodies. If a laceration is left untreated it can result in blindness.
- **Cataracts** - As with most breeds, cataracts are a common problem as the dog ages. For many breeders it is a disappointment that the cataracts typically develop long after the dog has already been bred.
- **Lens Luxations** - Lens luxations can be fairly common in the breed and result in secondary glaucoma
- **Glaucoma** - Glaucoma can also be a common issue amongst Griffons due to the breeds facial features and eye size.

Heat Stroke

Although Griffons have a shortened snout, heat stroke is not a major concern for them as it is with other flat-faced breeds. The breed's shortened muzzle may cause respiratory issues in extreme heat but overall they tolerate both hot and cold weather well. As with any breed, owners must use common sense and not leave them outdoors without protection from the elements or subject them to rigorous exercise during extreme temperatures.

Syringomyelia

Syringomyelia (SM) is a condition affecting the brain and spine, causing symptoms ranging from mild discomfort to severe pain and partial paralysis. Syringomyelia is characterised by fluid filled cavities within the spinal cord. SM occurs secondary to obstruction of cerebrospinal fluid (CSF) especially if that obstruction is at the foremen magnum. To date the condition has been also reported in Cavalier King Charles Spaniels, King Charles Spaniels, Yorkshire Terriers, Maltese Terriers, Chihuahuas, Miniature Dachshunds, Miniature/Toy Poodles, Bichon Frisé, Pugs, Shih Tzus, Pomeranians, Boston Terriers, French Bulldogs, a Pekingese, a Miniature Pinscher, mixbreeds, and a couple of cats.

Not all dogs with SM have clinical signs. The presence of signs is correlated to the width of the syrinx and extent of spinal cord dorsal horn damage. Syrinxes can progressively expand and a dog which is asymptomatic in early life may eventually become painful.

History

The three variations of this dog, the Brussels Griffon (Griffon bruxellois), the Belgian Griffon (Griffon belge), and the Petit Brabançon, all descend from an old type of dog called a *Smousje*, a rough coated, small terrier-like dog kept in stables to eliminate rodents, similar to the Dutch Smoushond. In Belgium coachmen were fond of their alert little *Griffons d'Ecurie* (wiry coated stable dogs) and in the 1800s, they bred their Griffons with imported toy dogs. Breeding with the Pug and King Charles Spaniel brought about the current breed type, but also brought the short black coat that led to the *Petits Brabançon*, which was originally a fault in the breed. The spaniels also brought the rich red and black and tan colour of the modern Griffon Bruxellois and Griffon Belge.

The Griffon Bruxellois grew in popularity in the late 1800s with both workers and noblemen in Belgium. The first Griffon Bruxellois was registered in 1883 in the first volume Belgium's kennel club studbook, the *Livre des Origines Saint-Hubert* (LOSH). The popularity of the breed was increased by the interest of Queen Marie Henriette, a dog enthusiast who visited the annual dog shows in Belgium religiously, often with her daughter, and became a breeder and booster of Griffon Bruxellois, giving them international fame and popularity. Many dogs were exported to other countries, leading to Griffon Bruxellois clubs in England (1897) and Brussels Griffon clubs in the U.S.A. (1945.)

The First World War and Second World War proved to be a disastrous time for the breed. War time is difficult on any dog breed, and the recovering numbers after the First World War were set back by increased vigilance in breeding away from faults such as webbed toes. By the end of the Second World War, Belgium had almost no native Griffon Bruxellois left, and it was only through the vigilance of dedicated breeders (in the U.K. particularly) that the breed survived at all.

The breed has never been numerous or popular, but had a brief vogue in the late 1950s, and now is generally an uncommon breed. There has been a recent increase in interest in the United States due to appearance of a Griffon in the movie, *As Good as It Gets*, and also because of a general increase in interest in toy dogs.

Griffon Bruxellois in popular culture

- In the film *As Good as It Gets* (1997), as Verdell, played by six Brussels Griffons, named Timer, Sprout, Debbie, Billy, Parfait, and Jill the star
- In the film *Gosford Park*, as Rolf Liechti's dog Kiki
- In the film *Sweet November*, as Sara's dog Ernie
- In the sitcom *Spin City*, as Carter's suicidal dog Rags, played by a smooth-coated Petit Brabançon named Wesley
- Monkey, owned by record label owner and deejay Sarah Lewitinn and named "Best Dog Owned by a Club Personality" by The Village Voice
- Tazzie owned by Stanely Dangerfield, appearing on the television show *The Good Companions*

- In the film *First Wives Club* owned by Diane Keaton's character.

See also

- Toy Group
- Companion Group
- Lap dog
- Dutch Smoushond

External links

- American Brussels Griffon Association [1]
- National Brussels Griffon Club [2]
- National Brussels Griffon Rescue, Inc. [3]
- The Brussels Griffon Forum [4]
- UK Griffon Bruxellois [5]

Cavalier King Charles Spaniel

The **Cavalier King Charles Spaniel** is a small breed of Spaniel-type dog, and is classed as a Toy dog by most Kennel Clubs. It is one of the most popular breeds in the United Kingdom. Since 2000, it has been growing in popularity in the United States. It is a smaller breed of Spaniel, and Cavalier adults are often the same size as adolescent dogs of other spaniel breeds. It has a silky coat and commonly an undocked tail. The breed standard recognizes four colours (Blenheim, Tricolour [black/white/tan], Black and Tan, and Ruby). The breed is generally friendly, affectionate and good with both children and other animals.

The King Charles had changed drastically in the late 1600s, when it was interbred with flat-nosed breeds. Until the 1920s, the Cavalier shared the same history as the smaller King Charles Spaniel. Breeders attempted to recreate what they considered to be the original configuration of the breed, a dog resembling Charles II's King Charles Spaniel of the Restoration.

Various health issues affect this particular breed, most notably mitral valve disease, which leads to heart failure. This will appear in most Cavaliers at some point in their lives and is the most common cause of death. The breed may also suffer from Syringomyelia, a malformation of the skull that reduces the space available for the brain. Cavaliers are also affected by ear problems, a common health problem among spaniels of various types, and they can suffer from such other general maladies as hip dysplasia, which are common across many types of dog breeds.

History

During the 16th century, a small type of spaniel was popular among the nobility in England. The people of the time believed that these dogs could keep fleas away, and some even believed that they could prevent forms of stomach illnesses. These dogs were sometimes called the "Spaniel Gentle" or "Comforter", as ladies taking a carriage ride would take a spaniel on their laps to keep them warm during the winter. Charles I kept a spaniel named Rogue while residing at Carisbrooke Castle, however it is Charles II that this breed is closely associated and it was said of him that "His Majesty was seldom seen without his little dogs". There is a myth that he even issued an edict that no spaniels of this type could be denied entry to any public place.

During the reign of King William III and Queen Mary II, the long nosed style of spaniel went out of fashion. The Pug was the favoured dog at the time in the Netherlands, and with William's Dutch origin, they became popular in England too. At this time interbreeding may have occurred with the Pug, or other flat nosed breeds, as the King Charles took on some Pug-like characteristics, but in any event the modern King Charles Spaniel emerged. In *The Dog* in 1852, Youatt was critical of the change in the breed:

During the early part of the 18th century, John Churchill, 1st Duke of Marlborough, kept red and white King Charles type spaniels for hunting. The duke recorded that they were able to keep up with a trotting horse. His estate was named Blenheim in honour of his victory at the Battle of Blenheim. Because of this influence, the red and white variety of the King Charles Spaniel and thus the Cavalier King Charles Spaniel became known as the Blenheim.

Attempts were made to recreate the original King Charles Spaniel as early as the turn of the 20th century, using the now extinct Toy Trawler Spaniels. These attempts were documented by Judith Blunt-Lytton, 16th Baroness Wentworth, in the book *"Toy Dogs and Their Ancestors Including the History And Management of Toy Spaniels, Pekingese, Japanese and Pomeranians"* published under the name of the "Hon. Mrs Neville Lytton" in 1911.

Divergence from King Charles Spaniel

In 1926, American Roswell Eldridge offered a dog show class prize of twenty-five pounds each as a prize for the best male and females of "Blenheim Spaniels of the old type, as shown in pictures of Charles II of England's time, long face, no stop, flat skull, not inclined to be domed, with spot in centre of skull." The breeders of the era were appalled, although several entered what they considered to be sub-par King Charles Spaniels in the competition. Eldridge died before seeing his plan come to fruition, but several breeders believed in what he said and in 1928 the first Cavalier club was formed. The first standard was created, based on a dog named "Ann's Son" owned by Mostyn Walker, and the The Kennel Club recognised the breed as "King Charles Spaniels, Cavalier type".

World War II caused a drastic setback to the breed, with the vast majority of breeding stock destroyed because of the hardship. For instance, in the Ttiweh Cavalier Kennel, the population of sixty dropped to three during the 1940s. Following the war, just six dogs would be the starting block from which all Cavaliers descend. These dogs were Ann's Son, his litter brother Wizbang Timothy, Carlo of Ttiweh, Duce of Braemore, Kobba of Kuranda and Aristide of Ttiweh. The numbers increased gradually, and in 1945 The Kennel Club first recognised the breed in its own right as the Cavalier King Charles Spaniel.

The history of the breed in America is relatively recent. The first recorded Cavalier living in America was brought from Britain in 1956 by W. Lyon Brown, together with Elizabeth Spalding and other enthusiasts, she founded the Cavalier King Charles Club USA which continues to the present day. In 1994, the American Cavalier King Charles Spaniel Club was created by a group of breeders to apply for recognition by the American Kennel Club. The Cavalier would go on to be recognised in 1997, and the ACKCSC became the parent club for Cavaliers.

Description

The Cavalier King Charles Spaniel is one of the largest toy breeds. Historically it was a lap dog, and modern day adults can fill a lap easily. Nonetheless, it is small for a spaniel, with fully grown adults comparable in size to adolescents of other larger spaniel breeds. Breed standards state that height of a Cavalier should be between with a proportionate weight between . The tail is usually not docked, and the Cavalier should have a silky coat of moderate length. Standards state that it should be free from curl, although a slight wave is allowed. Feathering can grow on their ears, feet, legs and tail in adulthood. Standards require this be kept long, with the feathering on the feet a particularly important aspect of the breed's features.

The Cavalier King Charles Spaniel and the English Toy Spaniel can be often confused with each other. In the United Kingdom, the English Toy Spaniel is called the King Charles Spaniel while in the United States, one of the colours of the Toy Spaniel is known as King Charles. The two breeds share similar history and only diverged from each other about 100 years ago. There are several major differences between the two breeds, with the primary difference being the size. While the Cavalier weighs on average between , the King Charles is smaller at . In addition their facial features while similar, are different, the Cavalier's ears are set higher and its skull is flat while the King Charles's is domed. Finally the muzzle length of the Cavalier tends to be longer than that of its King Charles cousin.

Colour

The breed has four recognized colours. Cavaliers which have rich chestnut markings on a pearly white background are known as Blenheim in honour of Blenheim Palace, where John Churchill, 1st Duke of Marlborough, raised the predecessors to the Cavalier breed in this particular colour. In some dogs there is a chestnut spot in the middle of the forehead: this is called the "blenheim" spot. Black and Tan are dogs with black bodies with tan highlights, particularly eyebrows, cheeks, legs and beneath the tail.

Black and Tan is referred to as "King Charles" in the King Charles Spaniel. Ruby Cavaliers should be entirely chestnut all over, although some can have some white in their coats which is considered a fault under American Kennel Club conformation show rules. The fourth colour is known as Tricolour, which is black and white with tan markings on cheeks, inside ears, on eyebrows, inside legs, and on underside of tail. This colour is referred to as "Prince Charles" in the King Charles Spaniel.

Popularity

According to statistics released by The Kennel Club, Cavaliers were the 6th most popular dog in the United Kingdom in 2007 with 11,422 registrations in a single year. Labrador Retrievers were the most popular with 45,079 registrations in that year. Their popularity is on the rise in America; in 1998 they were the 56th most popular breed but in both 2007 and 2008 they were the 25th most popular. They ranked higher in some individual US cities in the 2008 statistics, being eighth in both Nashville and Minneapolis-St.Paul, seventh in Boston, Atlanta and Washington D.C., and sixth in both New York City and San Francisco. In 2009, the Cavalier was the fourth most popular breed in Australia with 3,196 registrations behind only Labrador Retrievers, German Shepherd Dogs and Staffordshire Bull Terriers. In addition, there are also national breed clubs in Belgium, Canada, Czech Republic, Denmark, Finland, France, Germany, Italy, Netherlands, New Zealand, Norway, South Africa and Sweden.

Temperament

The breed is highly affectionate, playful, extremely patient and eager to please. As such, dogs of the breed are good with children and other dogs. Cavaliers are not shy about socializing with much larger dogs. They will adapt quickly to almost any environment, family, and location. Their ability to bond with larger and smaller dogs make them ideal in houses with more than one breed of dog as long as the other dog is trained. The breed is great with people of all ages, from children to seniors, making them a very versatile dog. Cavaliers rank 44th in Stanley Coren's *The Intelligence of Dogs*, being of average intelligence in working or obedience. Cavaliers are naturally curious and playful, but also enjoy simply cuddling up on a cushion or lap.

Cavaliers are active and sporting. They have an instinct to chase most things that move including while on busy streets, and so most Cavaliers will never become "street-wise". As they tend to regard all strangers as friends, members of the breed will usually never make a good guard dog. Spaniels have a strong hunting instinct and may endanger birds and small animals. However, owners have reported that through training their Cavaliers live happily with a variety of small animals including hamsters and gerbils.

Health

Cavaliers can often suffer from some serious genetic health problems, including early-onset mitral valve disease (MVD), the potentially severely painful syringomyelia (SM), hip dysplasia, luxating patellas, and certain vision and hearing disorders. As today's Cavaliers all descend from only six dogs, any inheritable disease present in at least one of the original founding dogs can be passed on to a significant proportion of future generations. This is known as the founder effect and is the likely cause of the prevalence of MVD in the breed. The health problems shared with King Charles Spaniels include mitral valve disease, luxating patella, and hereditary eye issues such as cataracts and retinal dysplasia.

Mitral valve disease

Nearly all Cavaliers eventually suffer from disease of the mitral valve, with heart murmurs which may progressively worsen, leading to heart failure. This condition is polygenic (affected by multiple genes), and therefore all lines of Cavaliers worldwide are susceptible. It is the leading cause of death in the breed. A survey by The Kennel Club of the United Kingdom showed that 42.8% of Cavalier deaths are cardiac related. The next most common causes are cancer (12.3%) and old age (12.2%). The condition can begin to emerge at an early age and statistically may be expected to be present in more than half of all Cavalier King Charles Spaniels by age 5. It is rare for a 10-year-old Cavalier not to have a heart murmur. While heart disease is common in dogs generally − one in 10 of all dogs will eventually have heart problems − mitral valve disease is generally (as in humans) a disease of old age. The "hinge" on the heart's mitral valve loosens and can gradually deteriorate, along with the valve's flaps, causing a heart murmur (as blood seeps through the valve between heartbeats) then congestive heart failure. The Cavalier is particularly susceptible to early-onset heart disease, which may be evident in dogs as young as one or two years of age. Veterinary geneticists and cardiologists have developed breeding guidelines to eliminate early-onset mitral valve disease in the breed, but it is unclear if a statistically significant number of breeders follow these guidelines. The chairperson of the UK CKCS Club has said that "There are many members who are still not prepared to health check their breeding stock, and of those who do, it would appear that many would not hesitate to breed from affected animals." The MVD breeding protocol recommends that parents should be at least 2.5 years old and heart clear, and their parents (i.e., the puppy's grandparents) should be heart clear until age 5.

Syringomyelia

Syringomyelia (SM) is a condition affecting the brain and spine, causing symptoms ranging from mild discomfort to severe pain and partial paralysis. It is caused by a malformation in the lower back of the skull which reduces the space available to the brain, compressing it and often forcing it out (herniating it) through the opening into the spinal cord. This blocks the flow of cerebral spinal fluid (CSF) around the brain and spine and increases the fluid's pressure, creating turbulence which in turn is believed to create fluid pockets, or syrinxes (hence the term syringomyelia), in the spinal cord. Syringomyelia is rare in most breeds but has become widespread in the Cavalier King Charles Spaniel, with international research samples in the past few years consistently showing over 90% of cavaliers have the malformation, and that between 30–70% have syrinxes. However, most dogs with syrinxes are not symptomatic. Although symptoms of syringomyelia can present at any age, they typically appear between six months and four years of age in 85% of symptomatic dogs, according to Clare Rusbridge, a research scientist. Symptoms include sensitivity around the head, neck, or shoulders, often indicated by a dog whimpering or frequently scratching at the area of his neck or shoulder. Scratching is often unilateral – restricted to one side of the body. Scratching motions are frequently performed without actually making physical contact with the body ("air scratching"). The scratching behavior appears involuntary and the dog frequently scratches while walking – without stopping – in a way that is very atypical of normal scratching ("bunny hopping"). Scratching typical of SM is usually worse when the dog is wearing a collar, is being walked on leash, or is excited, and first thing in the morning or at night.

Not all dogs with SM show scratching behavior. Not all dogs who show scratching behavior appear to suffer pain, though several leading researchers, including Dr Clare Rusbridge in the UK and Drs Curtis Dewey and Dominic Marino in the US, believe scratching in SM cavaliers is a sign of pain and discomfort and of existing neurological damage to the dorsal horn region of the spine. If onset is at an early age, a first sign may be scratching and/or rapidly appearing scoliosis. If the problem is severe, there is likely to be poor proprioception (awareness of body position), especially with regard to the forelimbs. Clumsiness and falling results from this problem. Progression is variable though the majority of dogs showing symptoms by age four tend to see progression of the condition.

A veterinarian will rule out basic causes of scratching or discomfort such as ear mites, fleas, and allergies, and then, primary secretory otitis media (PSOM – glue ear), as well as spinal or limb injuries, before assuming that a Cavalier has SM. PSOM can present similar symptoms but is much easier and cheaper to treat. Episodic Falling Syndrome can also present similar symptoms. An MRI scan is normally done to confirm diagnosis of SM (and also will reveal PSOM). If a veterinarian suspects SM he or she will recommend an MRI scan. Neurologists give scanned dogs a signed certificate noting its grade.

Episodic Falling (EF)

Episodic Falling is an "exercise-induced paroxysmal hypertonicity disorder" meaning that there is increased muscle tone in the dog and the muscles cannot relax. Except for severe cases, episodes will be in response to exercise, excitement or similar exertions. Although EF is often misdiagnosed as epilepsy, which typically results in loss of consciousness, the dog remains conscious throughout the episode. Severity of symptoms can range from mild, occasional falling to freezing to seizure-like episodes lasting hours. Episodes can become more or less severe as the dog gets older and there is no standard pattern to the attacks. The onset of symptoms usually occurs before five months but can appear at any age. It is similar to Scotty Cramp, a genetic disorder in Scottish Terriers.

Thrombocytopenia and macrothrombocytopenia

As many as half of all Cavalier King Charles Spaniels may have a congenital blood disorder called idiopathic asymptomatic thrombocytopenia, an abnormally low number of platelets in the blood, according to recent studies in Denmark and the United States. Platelets, or thrombocytes, are disk-shaped blood elements which aid in blood clotting. Excessively low numbers are the most common cause of bleeding disorders in dogs. The platelets in the blood of many Cavalier King Charles Spaniels are a combination of those of normal size for dogs and others that are abnormally oversized, or macrothrombocytes. Macrothrombocytosis also is a congenital abnormality found in at least a third of CKCSs. These large platelets function normally, and the typical Cavalier does not appear to experience any health problems due to either the size or fewer numbers of its platelets.

Hip and knee disorders

Hip dysplasia (HD) is a common genetic disease that affects Cavalier King Charles Spaniels. It is never present at birth and develops with age. Hip dysplasia is diagnosed by X-rays, but it is not usually evident in X-rays of Cavaliers until they mature. Even in adult spaniels with severe HD, X-rays may not always indicate the disease. In a series of evaluations by the Orthopedic Foundation for Animals, the Cavalier was ranked 78th worst out of 157 breeds. The worst affected breeds were the Bulldog, Pug and Dogue de Bordeaux.

Cavaliers can be subject to a genetic defect of the femur and knee called luxating patella. This condition is most often observed when a puppy is 4 to 6 months old. In the most serious cases, surgery may be indicated. The grading system for the patella runs from 1 (a tight knee), to 4 (a knee so loose that its cap is easily displaced). If a cavalier has a grade 1–2, physical rehabilitation therapy and exercise may reduce the grading and potentially avoid surgery. The grades 3–4 are most severe where surgery will most likely be needed to correct the problem to avoid the development of arthritis and lameness in the limb.

Eye problems

A disorder occasionally seen in Cavaliers is keratoconjunctivitis sicca, colloquially known as "dry eye". The usual cause of this condition is an autoimmune reaction against the dog's lacrimal gland (tear gland), reducing the production of tears. According to the Canine Inherited Disorders Database, the condition requires continual treatment and if untreated may result in partial or total blindness. This disorder can decrease or heal over time.

A 1999 study of Cavaliers conducted by the Canine Eye Registration Foundation showed that an average of 30% of all Cavalier King Charles Spaniels evaluated had eye problems. They include hereditary cataracts, corneal dystrophy, distichiasis, entropion, microphthalmia, progressive retinal atrophy, and retinal dysplasia.

Ear disorders

Primary Secretory Otitis Media (PSOM), also known as glue ear, consists of a highly viscous mucus plug which fills the dog's middle ear and may cause the tympanic membrane to bulge. PSOM has been reported almost exclusively in Cavaliers, and it may affect up to 40% of them. Because the pain and other sensations in the head and neck areas, resulting from PSOM, are similar to some symptoms caused by syringomyelia (SM), some examining veterinarians have mis-diagnosed SM in Cavaliers which actually have PSOM and not SM.

Cavalier King Charles Spaniels may be predisposed to a form of congenital deafness, which is present at birth, due to a lack of formation or early degeneration of receptors in the inner ear, although this is relatively rare. In addition, more recent studies have found Cavaliers that develop a progressive hearing loss, which usually begins during puppyhood and progresses until the dog is completely deaf, usually between the ages of three and five years. The progressive nature of this form of deafness in Cavaliers is believed to be caused by degeneration of the hearing nerve rather than the lack of formation or early degeneration of the inner ear receptors.

See also

- Companion dog
- Companion Dog Group
- Toy Group

Chihuahua (dog)

The " () is the smallest breed of dog and is named after the state of Chihuahua in Mexico. Chihuahuas are noted for their nervous temperament and diminutive appearance.

History

The Chihuahua's history is a puzzling one, as there are many theories surrounding their true origin. The Chihuahua was used in sacred rituals as they were considered holy to pre-Columbian Indian nations. They were also popular pets among the upper class. The breed draws its name from the Mexican State of Chihuahua, where the first specimens of the breed were discovered.

Some historians believe that the Chihuahua came from the island of Malta in the Mediterranean,. More evidence for this theory lies in European paintings of small dogs that resemble the Chihuahua. One of the most famous paintings is a fresco in the Sistine Chapel by Sandro Botticelli dated 1482. The painting, Scenes from the Life of Moses, shows a woman holding two tiny dogs with round heads, large eyes, big ears, and other characteristics similar to the Chihuahua. The painting was finished ten years before Columbus returned from the New World. It would have been impossible for Botticelli to have seen a Mexican dog, yet he depicted an animal strikingly similar to a Chihuahua.

Another theory suggests that the Chihuahua was brought to Mexico from China over 200 years ago. Supporters of this theory believe the Chinese were recognized for dwarfing plants and animals, and when rich Chinese merchants moved to Mexico, they brought Chihuahuas with them. The Aztecs had a little dog named the *Techichi*; however, analysis of the Chihuahua's mitochondrial DNA suggests that it is of Old World origin , such as from a European toy dog. The mitochondrial DNA analysis only looks at what is inherited from the mother; therefore the fathers of the Chihuahua could have been the *Techichi*.

Both folklore and archeological finds show that the breed originated in Mexico. The most common theory and most likely is that Chihuahuas are descended from the *Techichi*, a companion dog favored by the Toltec civilization in Mexico.

Historical records indicate that the *Techichi* hunted in packs. They can only be traced as far back as the ninth century but it is highly likely that this is the Chihuahua's native Mexican ancestor. Evidence of this is that the remains of dogs closely resembling, but slightly larger than the average Chihuahua have been found in such places as the Great Pyramid of Cholula, which dates back to the 2nd century BC and predates the 16th century. There is also evidence to suggest that the *Techichi* may predate the Mayans.

The Toltecs were conquered by the Aztecs, who believed that the *Techichi* held mystical powers. In terms of size, the present day Chihuahua is much smaller than its ancestors, a change thought to be due to the introduction of miniaturized Chinese dogs, such as the Chinese crested dog, into South America by the Spanish.

A progenitor of the breed was reputedly found in 1850 in old ruins near Casas Grandes in the Mexican state of Chihuahua from which the breed gets its name. The state borders on Texas, Arizona and New Mexico in the United States, where Chihuahuas first rose to prominence and were further developed. Since that time, the Chihuahua has remained consistently popular as a breed, particularly in America when the breed was first recognized by the American Kennel Club in 1904. Genetic tests place the Chihuahua with other modern breeds originating in the 1800s.

Description and standards

Breed standards for this dog do not generally specify a height, only a weight and a description of their overall proportions. As a result, height varies more than within many other breeds. Generally, the height ranges between six and ten inches. However, some dogs grow as tall as 12 to 15 inches (30 to 38 cm). Both British and American breed standards state that a Chihuahua must not weigh more than six pounds for conformation. However, the British standard also states that a weight of two to four pounds is preferred and that if two dogs are equally good in type, the more diminutive or smaller is preferred. The Fédération Cynologique Internationale (FCI) standard calls for dogs ideally between 1.5 and 3.0 kg (3.3 to 6.6 lbs.), although smaller ones are acceptable in the show ring. Pet-quality Chihuahuas (that is, those bred or purchased as companions rather than show dogs) often range above these weights, even above ten pounds if they have large bone structures or are allowed to become overweight. This does not mean that they are not purebred Chihuahuas; they do not meet the requirements to enter a conformation show. Oversized Chihuahuas are seen in some of the best, and worst, bloodlines. Typically the breed standard for both the long and short coat chihuahua will be identical except for the description of the coat...

Chihuahua breeders often use terms like miniature, teacup, tiny toy, apple headed, or deer headed, to describe puppies. These terms are not recognized by the breed standards and may be misleading.

Coat

The Kennel Club in the United Kingdom and the American Kennel Club in the United States only recognize two varieties of Chihuahua: the long-coat, and the smooth-coat, also referred to as short-haired. They are genetically the same breed. The term smooth-coat does not mean that the hair is necessarily smooth, as the hair can range from having a velvet touch to a whiskery feeling. Long-haired Chihuahuas are actually smoother to the touch, having soft, fine guard hairs and a downy undercoat, which gives them their fluffy appearance. Unlike many long-haired breeds, long-haired Chihuahuas require no trimming and minimal grooming. Contrary to popular belief, the long-haired breed also typically sheds less than their short-haired counterparts. It may take up to two or more years before a full long-haired coat develops. .

Colors

The American Kennel Club Chihuahua standard lists under color: "Any color-Solid, marked or splashed". This allows for all colors from solid blacks to solid whites, spotted, sabled, or a variety of other colors and patterns. A few examples are Fawn, Red, Cream, Chocolate, Blue, and Black. Merle coloring is a spotted coat. Patterns, all with or without white markings, include:

- Sable
- Irish spotting
- Dalmatian spotting
- Piebald spotting
- Extreme black spotting
- Brindle
- Masks
- Tan points
- Red
- White
- Black
- Merle
- Orange
- Fawn
- Tricolor
- Dark brown
- Blue
- extremely rare blue brindle

The merle coat pattern is not traditionally considered part of the breed standard. The United Kingdom Kennel Club decided in May 2007 not to register puppies with "Merle coat color in dogs" coloration due to the health risks associated with the gene responsible, and in December of that year formally amended the Breed Standard to say "Any color or mixture of colors but never merle (dapple)." The Fédération Cynologique Internationale, which represents the major kennel club of 84 countries also disqualified merle. Other countries' Kennel Clubs; including Canada, Australia, New Zealand, and Germany have also disqualified merle. However, in May 2008 the Chihuahua Club of America voted that merles will not be disqualified in the United States and they are fully registrable and able to compete in all American Kennel Club (AKC) events. Opponents of recognizing merle dogs in the breed standards suspect the coloration came about by modern genetic cross-breeding with other dogs, and not via natural genetic drift.

Classifying Chihuahua colors can be complicated due to the large number of possibilities. Examples would be a blue brindle or a chocolate and tan. Colors and patterns can combine and affect each other, resulting in a very high degree of variation. The classic Chihuahua color remains fawn. No color or pattern is considered more valuable than the others, although blue is considered rare.

Temperament

More than most other breeds, how a Chihuahua turns out depends mightily on the genetic temperament of his parents and grandparents (entire lines are social or antisocial) and how it is raised (socialization and training) when brought home.[1] A Chihuahua must be chosen with care, as the temperament of its owner(s) can make a difference in the temperament of the pup. Ill tempered Chihuahuas can be easily provoked to attack, and are therefore generally unsuitable for homes with small children. The AKC describes the breed as, "A graceful, alert, swift-moving little dog with saucy expression, compact, and with terrier-like qualities of temperament." The breed tends to be fiercely loyal to one particular owner and in some cases may become over protective of the person, especially around other people or animals, but may be attached to more. They do not always get along with other breeds, and tend to have a "clannish" nature, often preferring the companionship of other Chihuahuas over other dogs. These traits generally make them unsuitable for households with children that are not patient and calm.

Chihuahuas crave attention, affection, exercise and being petted. They can be hyper, but eager to please. They have a reputation as a "yappy" dog, which can be resolved with proper training. Chihuahuas with proper breeding are not "yappy"; the AKC standard calls for "a terrier-like attitude."

Health disorders

This breed requires expert veterinary attention in areas such as birthing and dental care. Chihuahuas are also prone to some genetic anomalies, often neurological ones, such as epilepsy and seizure disorders.

Chihuahuas, and other toy breeds, are prone to the sometimes painful disease, hydrocephalus. It is often diagnosed by the puppy having an abnormally large head during the first several months of life, but other symptoms are more noticeable (since "a large head" is such a broad description). Chihuahua puppies exhibiting hydrocephalus usually have patchy skull plates rather than a solid bone and typically are lethargic and do not grow at the same pace as their siblings. A true case of hydrocephalus can be diagnosed by a veterinarian, though the prognosis is grim.

Chihuahuas have moleras, or a soft spot in their skulls, and they are the only breed of dog to be born with an incomplete skull. The molera fills in with age, but great care needs to be taken during the first six months until the skull is fully formed. Some moleras do not close completely and will require extra care to prevent injury. Many veterinarians are not familiar with Chihuahuas as a breed, and mistakenly confuse a molera with hydrocephalus. The Chihuahua Club of America has issued a statement regarding this often deadly misdiagnosis. Chihuahuas can also be at risk for hypoglycemia, or low blood sugar, they are one of the only dogs to get diabetes. This is especially dangerous for puppies. Left unattended, hypoglycemia can lead to coma and death. This can be combated with frequent feedings (every three hours for very small or young puppies). Chihuahua owners should have a simple sugar supplement on hand to use in emergencies, such as, Nutri-Cal, Karo syrup or honey. These supplements can be rubbed on the gums and roof of the mouth to rapidly raise the blood sugar level. Signs of hypoglycemia include lethargy, sleepiness, low energy, uncoordinated walking, unfocused eyes and spasms of the neck muscles (or head pulling back or to the side). Chihuahuas are prone to eye infections or eye injury due to their large, round, protruding eyes and their relatively low ground clearance. Care should be taken to prevent visitors or children from poking the eyes. The eyes also water to remove dust or allergens that may get into the eye. Daily wiping will keep the eyes clean and prevent tear staining. Chihuahuas have a tendency to tremble but this is not a health issue, rather it takes place when the dog is stressed, excited or cold. One reason for this may be because small dogs have a higher metabolism than larger dogs and therefore dissipate heat faster. Due to this Chihuahuas often wear coats or sweaters when outside in the cold or in overly air-conditioned places. Chihuahuas often like to dig and snuggle down in blankets for sleeping.

Although figures often vary, as with any breed, the average lifespan range for a healthy Chihuahua is approximately 10 to 17 years.

Chihuahuas are sometimes picky eaters, and care must be taken to provide them with adequate nutrition. Chihuahuas could earn this reputation because they seem to find small unnoticed bits of food all day. Sometimes wet or fresh food can have the most appealing smell to these constant eaters. "They will eat when they are hungry" does not apply as Chihuahuas are prone to hypoglycemia and could be at a critical state if allowed to go too long without a meal. At the same time, care must be exercised not to overfeed them. Human food should be avoided. Due to their small size even tiny high fat or sugary treats can result in an overweight Chihuahua. Overweight Chihuahuas are susceptible to having an increased rate of joint injuries, tracheal collapse, chronic bronchitis, and shortened life span.

Chihuahuas are also known for a genetic condition called 'luxating Patella'. It's a genetic condition that can occur in all dogs, old or young, slim or overweight, particularly small dogs. In some dogs, the ridges forming the patellar groove are not shaped correctly, and a shallow groove is created. In a dog with shallow grooves, the patella will luxate (Slip out of place) sideways, especially toward the inside. This causes the leg to 'lock up' and will cause the chihuahua to hold its foot off the ground. When the patella luxates from the groove of the femur, it usually cannot return to its normal position until the quadriceps muscle relaxes and increases in length. This explains why the affected dog may be forced to hold his leg up for a few minutes or so after the initial displacement. While the muscles are contracted and the patella is luxated from its correct position, the joint is held in the flexed or bent position. The knee cap sliding across the femur can cause some pain, due to the bony ridges of the femur. Once out of position, the animal feels no discomfort and continues his activity.

See also

- Companion dog
- Companion Dog Group
- Toy Group
- Dogs in Mesoamerica

Chinese Crested Dog

The **Chinese crested dog** is a smaller (10–13 lbs) hairless breed of dog. Like most hairless dog breeds, the Chinese crested comes in two varieties, both with and without fur, which are born in the same litter: the **Hairless** and the **Powderpuff**.

Description

At first glance, the "Hairless", and "Powderpuff" varieties of Chinese crested Dogs appear to be two different breeds, but hairlessness is an incomplete dominant trait within a single breed. The Hairless has soft, humanlike skin, as well as tufts of fur on its paws ("socks") and tail ("plume") and long, flowing hair on its head ("crest"). In addition to being an incomplete dominant gene, the "hairless" gene has a prenatal lethal effect when homozygous. Zygotes affected with double hairless genes (1 in 4) never develop into puppies, and are reabsorbed in the womb. All hairless Cresteds are therefore heterozygous.

The Hairless variety can vary in amount of body hair. Fur on the muzzle, known as a beard, is not uncommon. A true Hairless often does not have as much furnishings (hair on the head, tail, and paws). The difference between a very hairy Hairless and a Powderpuff is that the Hairless has a single coat with hairless parts on the body, while the Powderpuff has a thick double coat. The skin of the Hairless comes in a variety of colors, ranging from a pale flesh to black. Hairless Cresteds often lack a full set of premolar teeth, but this is not considered a fault.

The look of the Powderpuff varies according to how it is groomed. When its fur is completely grown out on its face, it strongly resembles a terrier; however, the Powderpuff is usually shaved around the snout as a standard cut.

The amount of body hair on the hairless variety varies quite extensively, from the true hairless which has very little or no body hair and furnishings, to what is called a 'hairy hairless', which if left ungroomed often grows a near-full coat of hair. These hairy hairless are not a mix between powderpuffs and hairless Chinese cresteds, but are merely a result of a weaker expression of the variable Hairless gene. The mutation responsible for the hairless trait was identified in 2008.

One famous Chinese crested dog was the hairless purebred named Sam, was the winner of the World's Ugliest Dog Contest from 2003 to 2005. He died before he could compete in 2006. Other Chinese cresteds have finished high in the event as well.

Care

Both varieties require certain amounts of grooming. The Puffs have a very soft and fine double coat that requires frequent brushing to avoid matting. Although a Puff's coat does not continuously grow like that of some other breeds, it can grow to be quite long at full length. This breed has little to no shedding " (see Moult).

Maintenance of the Hairless variety's skin is similar to maintaining human skin—and as such it can be susceptible to acne, dryness, and sunburn. Hypoallergenic or oil-free moisturizing cream can keep the skin from becoming too dry when applied every other day or after bathing. Burning can occur in regions that lend themselves to strong UV-rays, especially in lighter-skinned dogs. Many owners apply baby sunscreen to their pets before spending time in strong sun. Some Cresteds have skin allergies to Lanolin, so be cautious when using any products that contain it.

Unless the dog is a "True" Hairless (one with virtually no hair growth on non-extremities), trimming and/or shaving is often performed to remove excess hair growth.

The Chinese crested is further distinguished by its *hare foot*, (having more elongated toes) as opposed to the *cat foot* common to most other dogs. Because of this the quicks of Cresteds run deeper into their nails, so care must be taken not to trim the nails too short to avoid pain and bleeding.

Health

The crested is not affected by many of the congenital diseases found in toy breeds. They are, however, prone to some of the conditions below.

Cresteds have what is called a "primitive mouth". This means that most of their teeth are pointy like their canines. Hairless varieties of the Cresteds can be prone to poor dentition. Poor dentition may include missing or crowded teeth and teeth prone to decay when not properly cared for. Most dogs of the Puff variety have few, if any, dental defects.

Eyes are a concern within the breed, having at least two forms of progressive retinal atrophy (PRA) which can eventually lead to blindness. For one of these forms of PRA, there exists a genetic test, prcd-PRA. Since this test can only reveal the existence of affected or carrier status of this one form of PRA, breeders and owners of the breed should still have regular eye exams by veterinary ophthalmologists.

Along with Kerry Blue Terriers, Cresteds can develop canine multiple system degeneration (CMSD) also called progressive neuronal abiotrophy (PNA) in Kerry Blue Terriers. This is a progressive movement disorder that begins with cerebellar ataxia [1] between 10 and 14 weeks of age. After 6 months of age, affected dogs develop difficulty initiating movements and fall frequently. The gene responsible has been mapped to canine chromosome 1.

As with all other toy breeds, the Cresteds can be prone to patellar luxation. This inheritable condition is caused by shallow knee joints (stifles) and results in kneecaps that pop out of place. Its onset is often at a young age, and can cause temporary to permanent lameness based on the severity. Breeders should have their stock certified free of patellar luxation. Many countries' kennel clubs maintain a centralised registry for health results.

Allergy and autoimmune diseases have been observed in the breed. The severity of these ailments, which can lead to the premature death of the dog, means this is something breeders need to take seriously in order to avoid this becoming a problem for the breed.

The lifespan of a Chinese crested dog can be very long. Many Cresteds live 12 to 14 years or more.

History

Although hairless dogs have been found in many places in the world, it is unlikely that the origins of the modern Chinese crested are in China. In the 1920s, Debora Wood created the "Crest Haven" kennel and began to purposefully breed and record the lineages of her Chinese crested dogs. The famous burlesque dancer Gypsy Rose Lee also bred Chinese cresteds, and upon her death her dogs were incorporated into Crest Haven. These two lines were the true foundation of every Chinese crested alive today. Ms. Wood also founded the American Hairless Dog Club in 1959, which was eventually incorporated into the American Chinese crested Club (ACCC) in 1978. The ACCC became the U.S. parent club for the breed when the Chinese crested was recognized by the American Kennel Club thirteen years later, in 1991.

The Chinese crested was officially recognised by the Fédération Cynologique Internationale in 1987, by The Kennel Club (UK) in 1981, by the American Kennel Club in 1991, and by the Australian National Kennel Council in 1995.

The Chinese crested breed, either in purebred form or as a cross with chihuahua, has won eight World's Ugliest Dog Contests.

Breeding

The Hairless allele (the wild type) is a dominant (and homozygous prenatal lethal) trait, while the Powderpuff allele acts as a simple recessive trait in its presence. Zygotes that receive two copies of the Hairless allele will never develop into puppies. Thus all Chinese cresteds carry at least one copy of the Powderpuff allele.

The Powderpuff trait cannot be bred out because it is carried by all Chinese cresteds (even the hairless ones). All Hairless Chinese crested have the ability to produce Powderpuff puppies, even when they are bred to another Hairless. On the other hand, Powderpuffs bred to another Powderpuff can never produce hairless puppies, since they do not carry the Hairless gene.

In popular culture

- Peek from *Cats & Dogs*
- Fluffy from *102 Dalmatians*

See also

- Companion dog
- Companion Dog Group
- Toy Group
- Lap dog
- Xoloitzcuintli

King Charles Spaniel

The **King Charles Spaniel** (also known as the **English Toy Spaniel**) is a breed of small dog of the Spaniel type. The similar Cavalier King Charles Spaniel is a different breed. The Cavalier is slightly larger, has a flat head and a longer nose, while the "Charlie" is smaller, has a domed head and flat face.

Description

The English Toy Spaniel is a compact, cobby and essentially square toy dog possessed of a short-nosed, domed head, a merry and affectionate demeanor and a silky, flowing coat. The ears of the King Charles Spaniel are very long and set low and close to the head, fringed with heavy feathering.

Coat

Like its larger cousin, the Cavalier King Charles Spaniel, the King Charles Spaniel has a silky, often slightly wavy coat. It tends to be shorter than that of Cavaliers.

This breed also comes in the same color varieties as the Cavalier: Blenheim (brown-and-white), Prince Charles (tricolor), King Charles (black-and-tan), and Ruby (solid red). Originally, each of these color patterns was regarded as a separate breed, but in the late 1800s the four varieties were consolidated into a single breed.

The American Kennel Club has two classes: English Toy Spaniel (B/PC) (Blenheim and Prince Charles) and English Toy Spaniel (R/KC).

History

Toy spaniels were a favourite pet lap dog in Europe, with each family having its favourite. Charles II of England, Scotland and Ireland (1630 – 1685) was very fond of this type of dog, which is why the dogs of today carry his name, although there is no evidence that today's breed descended from his particular dogs. With the expansion of trade in the 17th and 18th centuries, Pugs and other dogs arrived from other parts of the world and became popular pets; this led to breeding with the spaniel lap dogs. The ancestry of the pug is seen in the shorter muzzle of the King Charles Spaniel.

In a 19th century book on British dogs, it is described how during the breed as was then was sometimes called "Melitei", which could imply that they came from Malta. However, the book thoroughly rubbishes any such claim and explains that the name didn't stick.

In 1903, The Kennel Club attempted to amalgamate the King James (black and tan), Prince Charle (tricolour), Blenheims and Ruby spaniels into a single breed called the Toy Spaniel. The Toy Spaniel Club which oversaw those separate breeds strongly objected, and the argument was only resolved following the intervention of King Edward VII who made it clear that he preferred the name "King Charles Spaniel".

Health

The King Charles Spaniel may have health problems such as heart defects (mitral valve disease, or MVD, is endemic in this breed as well as Cavalier King Charles Spaniels), eye problems, patellar luxation (kneecap slipping) and fused toes, which can cause incorrectly grown toenails. They are also one of the breeds identified with an incidence of the potentially serious neurological condition syringomyelia and have a significant occurrence of hydrocephalus. They tend to live 10 to 12 years.

The King Charles Spaniel and the Cavalier King Charles Spaniel have similar health issues. See the Cavalier King Charles Spaniel health section for more information.

See also

- Japanese Chin
- Pekingese
- Companion dog
- Companion Dog Group
- Toy Group

Havanese

The **Havanese** is a breed of dog of the Bichon type developed from the now extinct Bichon Tenerife, which was introduced to the Canary Islands by the Spanish. They are playful dogs and great with children and other animals. They are curious and friendly small dogs, bred to be companions and easily trainable. Havanese have a clown-like personality and are known to "hop" rather than run. They are highly adaptable to any environment and their only desire is to be with their humans.

Description

Appearance

The Havanese, while a toy dog, is hardy and sturdy and does not appear fragile or overly delicate. Weight is 8-17 pounds and height 8½ -11½ inches (216 to 292 mm), with the ideal between 9 and 10.5 inches (229 and 267 mm), at the withers. The height is slightly less than the length from point of shoulder to point of buttocks, which should give the dog the appearance of being slightly longer than tall. A unique aspect of the breed is the top line, which rises slightly from withers to rump, creating a back that is straight but not level. This breed is renowned for their unusually small tongue and flashy but not too reaching gait, giving the Havanese a sprightly, agile appearance.

Havanese have dark, round eyes. The ears are medium length, well feathered and should always hang down. The tail curves over the back at rest and is covered with a long plume of fur. Havanese are non shedding and hypoallergenic, great for people with dog allergies because they have little to no dander. Their coat should be brushed daily with failure to do so resulting in mats. Many pet owners clip their dogs into a 1-2 inch long "puppy cut" for ease of maintenance. Their hair, designed for Cuban heat, serves no protection during cold weather, so they are dogs for which one would buy a sweater. If they go out in the snow, ice clumps will stick between their paw pads; just rinse off in warm water or buy booties. When you give them a bath, make sure to dry them. Some in shorter clips can blot and air dry, but most will need to be blown dry. Use high air but low heat to protect their sensitive skin. Hot air can damage the skin.

The key word for the Havanese is "natural." The American Kennel Club standard notes "his character is essentially playful rather than decorative" and the Havanese, when shown, should reflect that, generally looking like a toy in size only, but more at home with playing with children or doing silly tricks than being pampered and groomed on a silk pillow. The breed standards note that except for slight clipping around the feet to allow for a circular foot appearance, and unnoticeable trimming around eyes and groin for hygienic purposes, they are to be shown untrimmed; any further trimming, back-combing, or other fussing is against type and will not be allowed to the point of precluding placement in dog shows. That includes undocked tails, uncropped ears. The American Kennel Club standard expressly forbids topknots, as the hair provided a degree of protection from the Cuban sun;

two small braids, held with plain bands and never bows, are also allowed in the AKC standard, as some dogs have too much hair to be reasonably kept in their face.

Color

Although there are a few arguments on whether the original Havanese were all white or of different colors, modern Havanese are acceptable in all coat colors and patterns. All colored dogs should have a black nose and black pigment around the eyes, with the exception of chocolate (brown) dogs, which may have dark brown pigment on their nose instead. The current American Kennel Club standard does not provide for Blue (slate blue-grey in color, different from silver) dogs; the standard allows for all colors and combination of colors to be allowed, but a blue dog will always have blue pigment, and the current standard expressly allows for only black or chocolate pigment.

Coat

The coat is long, soft, light, and silky. Havanese, like other Bichons and related dogs like Poodles, have a coat that catches hair and dander internally, and needs to be regularly brushed out.

Havanese are supposed to have a slightly wavy, profuse, double coat. However, unlike other double coated breeds, the Havanese outer coat is neither coarse nor overly dense, but rather soft and light with a slightly heavier undercoat. Not all Havanese have coats that match the standard. Havanese coats are supposed to be very soft, like unrefined silk (compared to the Maltese coat, which feels like refined silk). However, in some dogs the coat can become too silky, looking oily. On the other end of the spectrum, Havanese coats can be too harsh, giving a "frizzy" appearance. The coat should always be soft to the touch - never harsh, coarse, or cottony.

Because of the tropical nature of the Havanese, the thick coat is light and designed to act as a sunshade and cooling agent for the little dog on hot days. This means that the Havanese does need protection against cold winter days, in spite of the warm look of their fur.

The coat can be shown naturally brushed out, or corded, a technique which turns the long coat into "cords" of fur, similar to what dreadlocks are in humans. This corded look may be difficult to achieve for the first timer, so it is always recommended that someone interested in cording their Havanese consults someone who has done it before.

A havanese's coat can come in many colors such as, the most common, white and brown, and the least common, black.

Temperament

The Havanese has a playful, friendly temperament unlike other toy dog breeds. It is at home with young children and other pets and is rarely shy or nervous around new people. Clever and active, they will solicit attention by performing tricks. The breed does not require a lot of exercise.

The Havanese is a very people-oriented dog, often following their humans around the house. They are not overly possessive of their people and do not suffer aggression or jealousy towards other dogs, pets, or humans.

Their love of children stems from their days as the playmate of small children. Unlike most toy dogs, who are too delicate, nervous or aggressive to tolerate the often clumsy play of children, the Havanese, with care, is a cheerful companion to even younger children, and this is no small part of its growing popularity around the world.

Havanese have been known to eat only when they have company. If its person leaves the room, the dog will grab a mouthful of food and follow its "person", dropping the food and consuming it one morsel at a time in the room its person goes to.

Havanese are true "dogs", loving to play whenever the owner wants to. They calm down quickly when prompted to do so by their owners. They have excellent noses and are easily trained to play "find it," where the owner hides a treat and the Havanese sniffs it out until the treat is discovered. This is a highly trainable dog. They tend to jump up and down when they are given a tasty treat.

These are natural companion dogs: gentle and responsive. They become very attached to their humans and are excellent with children. Affectionate, playful and intelligent, they are very sociable, easy to obedience train and get along well with other dogs. They are sensitive to the tone of your voice and harsh punishment is unnecessary. Havanese have a long reputation as circus dogs because they learn quickly and enjoy doing things for people. The Fédération Cynologique Internationale standard notes that "he is easy to train as alarm dog." It is best to teach them not to bark unnecessarily while they are still young to prevent it from becoming a habit. Havanese can be good alarm dogs, alerting when a visitor arrives, but quick to welcome the guest once you welcome them. Since they are naturally curious, friendly, and people-oriented, they do not do well as guard dogs. Some may exhibit a degree of shyness around strangers, but this is not characteristic of the breed.

Health

Havanese are generally healthy and sturdy, living 14 to 19 years. Like other pure breeds, genetically-linked disorders are common due to the small genetic pool from which they owe their ancestry. Havanese organizations, such as the Havanese Club of America, monitor genetic issues to prevent propagation within the breed.

Havanese suffer primarily from liver disease, heart disease, cataracts and retinal dysplasia. Havanese sometimes tear and may develop brown tear stains, especially noticeable on white or light coats.

History

As part of the Cuban Revolution, trappings of aristocracy were culled, including the pretty but useless fluffy family dogs of the wealthy land owners. As upper-class Cubans fled to the United States, few were able to bring their dogs or had the inclination to breed them. When Americans became interested in this rare and charming dog in the 1970s, the US gene pool was only 11 animals.

With dedicated breeding, the acquisition of some new dogs internationally, the Havanese has made a huge comeback and is one of the fastest growing registration of new dogs in the American Kennel Club (AKC) (+42% in 2004). They have also acquired a certain level of trendiness due to rarity, temperament, and publicity by such famous owners as Barbara Walters. The Havanese is recognized by major registries in the English-speaking world. In addition to the American Kennel Club, it is recognized by The Kennel Club (UK), the Australian National Kennel Council, the New Zealand Kennel Club, the Canadian Kennel Club, the United Kennel Club (US), and was recognized as *Bichon Havanais*, breed number 250, by the Fédération Cynologique Internationale in 2006. It also may be recognized some of minor registries and internet based clubs and dog registry "businesses."

Havanese at work

Because of the cheerful and readily trained nature, they are used for a variety of jobs involving the public, including:

- Therapy dogs
- Assistance dogs, such as signal dogs for the hearing impaired.
- Performing dogs
- Mold and termite detection
- Tracking

Havanese also compete in a variety of dog sports, such as

- Dog agility
- Flyball
- Musical canine freestyle
- Obedience training

Care

Havanese have several specific considerations for their care that a prospective owner should keep in mind. The profuse coat requires daily grooming. If not showing the dog, it can be trimmed shorter to require less brushing. Their paws need trimming to allow traction on smooth floors. Some develop tear staining. Please consult with your veterinarian for options of how red yeast problems can be diminished or eliminated.

With their drop ears, they need to have their ears cleaned and ear hair removed to help prevent ear infections.

The Havanese is not a yappy dog, but will alert its owners to approaching people. Usually acknowledging that you have heard their alert is enough to make them cease. Some have strong attachment issues, known by their owners as "velcro dogs," following household members everywhere, even into the bathroom.

See also

- Bichon
- Lap dog
- Rare breed (dog)
- Companion dog
- Companion Dog Group
- Toy Group

External links

- American Kennel Club Havanese Page [1]
- Havanese Club of America [2]
- Havanese Fanciers of Canada (Canadian Kennel Club parent club of the Havanese Breed) [3]
- Animal Planet video on Havanese [4]

Havanese Rescue organizations:

- Havanese Angel League Organization; US based; purchases from puppy mills to rescue [5]
- Havanese Rescue, Inc.; US based; a charity despite the name "Inc." [6]
- Havanese Fanciers of Canada Rescue; Canada Based; Rescued dogs are provided with the attention, care and medical treatment necessary, including spay/neutering, until permanent homes can be found. [7]

Italian Greyhound

The **Italian Greyhound** is a small breed of dog of the sight hound type, sometimes called an "I.G.", or "Iggy" for short.

Description

Appearance

The Italian Greyhound is the smallest of the sighthounds, typically weighing about and standing about tall at the withers. Though they are in the "toy" group based on their weight, they are larger than other dogs in the category due to their slender bodies, so owners must be careful when sizing clothing or accommodations.

The Italian Greyhound's chest is deep, with a tucked up abdomen, long slender legs and a long neck that tapers down to a small head. The face is long and pointed, like a full sized greyhound. Overall, they look like "miniature" Greyhounds, though many Italian Greyhound owners dispute the use of the term "miniature Greyhound", in reference to the breed itself. By definition of the American Kennel Club - they are true genetic greyhounds, with a bloodline extending back over 2000 years. Their current small stature is a function of selective breeding. Their gait is distinctive and should be high stepping and free, rather like that of a horse. They are able to run at top speed with a double suspension gallop, and can achieve a top speed of up to .

The color of the coat is a subject of much discussion. For The Kennel Club (UK), the American Kennel Club, and the Australian National Kennel Council, parti colored Italian Greyhounds are accepted, while the Fédération Cynologique Internationale standard for international shows allows white only on the chest and feet.

The modern Italian Greyhound's appearance is a result of breeders throughout Europe, particularly Austrian, German, Italian, French and British breeders, making great contributions to the forming of this breed. The Italian Greyhound should resemble a small Greyhound, or rather a Sloughi, though they are in appearance more elegant and graceful.

Temperament

The Italian Greyhound is affectionate and makes a good companion dog. The breed is excellent for families and enjoys the company of people. While they are excellent with children, the breed's slim build and short coat make them somewhat fragile, and injury can result from rough or careless play with children under the age of 12.

Because they are sight hounds and love to run, Italian Greyhound must never be walked outside off-leash. Even well-trained Italian Greyhounds are known to bolt into traffic despite their owner's commands to stop.

The breed is equally at home in the city or the country, although they tend to do best in spacious areas. They are fast, agile and athletic. Like any dog, daily exercise is a must for a happier, well-adjusted pet. Italian greyhounds love to run. The young dog is often particularly active, and this high level of activity may lead them to attempt ill-advised feats of athleticism that can result in injury. Due to their size, and in some lineages poor bone density, they are prone to broken legs which can be expensive to repair.

In general the Italian Greyhound is intelligent, but they often have a "what's in it for me" attitude and do not exactly throw themselves into training with great excitement, so patience, firmness, gentleness, and reward in training seem to work best. They are also known for their mischievous ingenuity. Despite a high center of gravity, they can easily walk upright on their hind legs to reach items up on tables. They can also jump surprisingly high (some over 1.5 m vertically) to reach high-up items of interest to them, including leaping atop kitchen counter-tops from the floor.

Italian Greyhounds make reasonably good watchdogs, as they bark at unfamiliar sounds. They may also bark at passers-by and other animals. However, they should not be considered "true" guard dogs as they are often aloof with strangers and easily spooked to run. They often get along well with other dogs and cats they are raised with.

Due to their slim build and extremely short coat, Italian Greyhounds are at times reluctant to go outside in cold or wet weather, so some owners lay old newspaper on the floor near an exit so their pets can relieve themselves. Some respond well to dog-litter training as well. This breed tends to gravitate to warm places, curl up with other dogs or humans, or burrow into blankets and under cushions for warmth. Some smaller Italian Greyhounds are adept at burrowing into difficult places (e.g. pillowcases, laundry baskets containing warm clothes) as the breed has a strong affinity for warmth. Care must be taken near heat sources, such as fireplaces, baseboard heaters and electric space heaters as the dog may choose to sit dangerously close to them, especially during winter when ambient indoor temperatures are generally lower.

As gazehounds, Italian Greyhounds instinctively hunt by sight and have an extremely high predator drive. Owners of Italian Greyhounds typically keep their dogs leashed at all times when not in an enclosed area to avoid the risk of even a well-behaved pet breaking away at high speed after a small animal. Also, a short leash is highly suggested to owners due to reports of animals breaking their own necks when running a full lead mounted to the ground or a wall. Sometimes a dog harness is a good option; since the IG has a tapering neck and small head, they can often "slip" their collar and leash. Because of their frame, it is important to select a harness especially designed for this breed; a regular harness could dislocate their shoulder. This can also be used to avoid the above-mentioned neck injury if your dog is prone to bolting. It also gives the dog the freedom of a long leash.

Owners of Italian Greyhounds should be extremely mindful of any unknown dogs, no matter what size, because Italian Greyhounds can be extremely territorial, and may even "have a go" at any larger unknown dogs on their property.

Grooming

Dogs of this breed have an extremely short and almost odorless coat that requires little more than an occasional bath, but a wipe-down with a damp cloth is recommended after walks as seeds, burrs and floating dust in the air can get into the coat and irritate the skin. Shedding is typical as of other breeds, but the hair that is shed is extremely short and fine and is easily vacuumed.

Oral

The teeth of an Italian Greyhound should be brushed daily. Their scissor-bite and thin jaw bones make them susceptible to periodontal disease, which can be avoided with good dental care. Daily brushing has been shown to be very beneficial as well as regular dental cleanings from the vet.

Health

Health problems that can be found in the breed:

- Epilepsy
- Legg-Perthes disease (degeneration of the hip)
- Patellar Luxation (slipped stifles)
- von Willebrand disease (vWD) (Bleeding disorder)
- Progressive retinal atrophy (PRA)
- Color dilution alopecia (hair loss in dilute pigmented dogs, i.e.: blues, blue fawns, etc)
- Leg Breaks (most common under the age of 2)
- Cataracts
- Vitreous degeneration
- Liver shunts
- Autoimmune hemolytic anemia
- Periodontal disease, gum recession, early tooth loss, bad tooth enamel
- Hypothyroidism, Autoimmune Thyroid Disease (Hashimoto's disease)

Responsible breeders will routinely check their dogs for the onset of various inherited disorders, these commonly include (but are not limited to): CERF [1] examinations on eyes, OFA [2] patellar examinations, OFA [2] thyroid function panels, von Willebrand's factor, OFA [2] hip and Legg-Perthes disease x-rays, and others.In research by the Ortheopedic Foundation for Animals, the Italian Greyhound was found to be the least affected by hip dysplasia out of 157 breeds. Tests were conducted on 169 individual Italian Greyhounds, of which none were found to have hip dyplasia and 59.2% scored excellent on their hip evaluations.

History

The name of the breed is a reference to the breed's popularity in Renaissance Italy. Mummified dogs very similar to the Italian Greyhound (or small Greyhounds) have been found in Egypt, and pictorials of small Greyhounds have been found in Pompeii, and they were probably the only accepted companion-dog there. As an amusing aside the expression 'Cave Canem' (Beware of the dog) was a warning to visitors, not that the dogs would attack but to beware of damaging, tripping over or stepping on the small dogs. Dogs similar to Italian Greyhounds are recorded as having been seen around Emperor Nero's court in Rome in the first century AD.

Although the small dogs are mainly companionship dogs they have in fact been used for hunting rats or mice, often in combination with hunting falcons.

The Italian Greyhound is the smallest of the family of gaze hounds (dogs that hunt by sight). The breed is an old one and is believed to have originated more than 4,000 years ago in the countries now known as Greece and Turkey. This belief is based on the depiction of miniature greyhounds in the early decorative arts of these countries and on the archaeological discovery of small greyhound skeletons. By the Middle Ages, the breed had become distributed throughout Southern Europe and was later a favorite of the Italians of the sixteenth century, among whom miniature dogs were in great demand. Sadly, though, 'designer' breeders tried, and failed, to make the breed even smaller by crossbreeding it with other breeds of dogs. This only led to mutations with deformed skulls, bulging eyes and dental problems. The original Italian Greyhound had almost disappeared when groups of breeders got together and managed to return the breed to normal. From this period onward the history of the breed can be fairly well traced as it spread through Europe, arriving in England in the seventeenth century.

Miscellaneous

Italian Greyhounds in the arts

The grace of the breed has prompted several artists to include the dogs in paintings, among others Velázquez, Pisanello and Giotto.

The breed has been popular with royalty throughout, among the best known royal aficionados were Mary Stuart, Queen Anne, Queen Victoria, Catherine The Great, Frederick the Great and the Norwegian Queen Maud.

Italian Greyhounds in popular culture

- Nelly from the film *Good Boy!* is an Italian Greyhound played by "Motif" and "Imp".
- The American rock band Shellac named their fourth album *Excellent Italian Greyhound* in reference to drummer Todd Trainer's pet Italian Greyhound, Uffizi.
- The 3.5 Edition of the Player's Handbook for Dungeons & Dragons features a sketch of an Italian Greyhound under its description for "handle animal."
- New York Alternative Rock band Interpol's former bass guitar player Carlos Dengler owns an Italian Greyhound named Gaius.

Activities

Some Italian Greyhounds enjoy dog agility. The breed's lithe body and its love of action enable it to potentially do well at this sport, although not many Italian Greyhounds participate and their natural inclination is for straight-out racing rather than for working tightly as a team with a handler on a technical course.

Lure coursing is another activity well-fitted to the Italian Greyhound, and they seem to enjoy it tremendously. Although the Italian Greyhound is a very fast dog, it is not as well suited to racing as its larger cousin. Regardless, many Italian Greyhounds participate in amateur straight-track and oval-track racing.

External links

- Italian Greyhound Club of America [3]
- Italian Greyhound Society of the UK [4]

See also

- Hound
- Companion dog
- Companion Dog Group
- Toy Group
- Lap dog

Japanese Chin

The **Japanese Chin** (狆), also known as the **Japanese Spaniel**) is the dog of Japanese royalty. A lap dog and companion dog, this toy breed has a distinctive heritage.

Description

Appearance

Japanese Chin stand about 20 to 27 cm (8 to 11 in) in height at the withers and weight can vary from a low of 4 lbs to a high of 20 lbs, with an average of 7 to 9 pounds being the most common. The American Kennel Club and the Fédération Cynologique Internationale give no weight requirement for the Chin.

Temperament

This breed is considered one of the most cat-like of the dog breeds in attitude: it is alert, intelligent, and independent, and it uses its paws to wash and wipe its face. Other cat-like traits include their preference for resting on high surfaces such as the backs of sofas and chairs, their ability to walk across a coffee table without disturbing an item, and some of the surprising places their owners often find them in. They rank 62nd in Stanley Coren's The Intelligence of Dogs, being of fair working/obedience intelligence. A companion dog, it is loving and loyal to its owner and typically happy to see other people, though a few are distrustful of strangers. Chin prefer familiar surroundings, but do quite well in new situations and are often used as therapy dogs because of this trait and their love of people. Very early socialization of Chin puppies leads to a more emotionally well-balanced Chin that is more accepting of different situations and people.

The Chin will bark for the purpose of alerting the household to the arrival of a visitor or something out of the ordinary, but are otherwise very quiet.

Chin were bred for the purpose of loving and entertaining their people. While typically a calm little dog, they are well known for performing many enjoyable antics such as the "Chin Spin," in which they turn in rapid circles; dancing on their hind legs while pawing their front feet, clasped together, in the air; and, some even "sing," a noise that can range from a low trill to a higher, almost operatic quality noise, and which sounds much like "boooo."

Health

This breed's flattened face contributes to a few Chin suffering from breathing and heart problems, as is common with brachycephalic breeds. Because they are a brachycephalic breed, temperature extremes (particularly heat) should be avoided. Luxating patellas (knees) and heart murmurs are other genetically predisposed conditions. The oversized eyes are easily scratched and corneal scratches or more serious ulcerations can result. Mild scratches benefit from topical canine antibacterial ointment specifically for eye application; more serious injury or ulcerations require urgent medical care. The Chin, as with most small breed dogs, can also have a risk of hypoglycemia when under the age of 6 months; this concern can continue in Chin that mature at 4 to 5 pounds or less. Some Chin do have seasonal allergies.

Care

The Chin's coat requires nothing more than brushing or combing once every day or two to maintain its appearance, with special attention being given to the area under the ears and legs and to the skirt; they have no coat odor and do not require frequent bathing. Chin are single-coated and single-hair shedders, much like people, and it is very seldom one will find a Chin with an undercoat. Occasionally, a Chin will have a light blowing of their coat once a year. Without fiber in the diet, they may need to have their anal glands expressed bimonthly. The oversized eye orbits contribute to moisture about the face and the skin folds in and around the nose and flattened facial area can trap moisture and cause fungal problems. The face should be occasionally wiped with a damp cloth and the folds cleaned with a cotton swab.

Diet is an important factor in the health and condition of the Chin, with many Chin being very sensitive or allergic to corn. Maintaining a Chin on a high quality kibble that contains no corn will do much to avoid skin and allergy conditions.

Due to low exercise requirements, the Chin makes a perfect condominium or apartment pet. The use of "housetraining pads" is recommended. The Chin is very easy to housetrain with many learning the use of a doggie door (some as young as 8 weeks old) in a day's time with assistance from their person. Similarly, it is very easy to train them to the housetraining pads, or even a litter box, by limiting their area until they have mastered use of the pads or litter box.

History

The true origin of the Chin remains a matter of controversy. It is widely agreed that the source breed for the Japanese Chin originated in China.

These dogs were brought over to Japan around 732. Some maintain the ancestors of these dogs first appeared in Japan around the year 732, as gifts from the rulers of Korea, while others maintain that they were given as gifts to the Empress of Japan as early as the mid-6th century to 7th century, and even some saying they came to Japan as recently as around the year 1000.

The Japanese Chin is truly a "Japanese" creation in that it reflects Japanese sensibilities.

The Japanese created a breed so distinct from other dogs, that in Japan it was considered something different, distinct from a "dog" which was considered a working/helper animal whereas the Japanese Chin was considered strictly for pleasurable companionship.

Its distinct appearance and personality eventually captured the hearts of Japanese Royalty and resulted in ownership being restricted to those of royal and noble blood.

Each noble house bred to their own standards. Because of this, there are many variations of the Chin in any area from size to coat density, eye set, personality, whether they are compact and well-muscled or slender-boned and fragile in appearance, etc.

Once introduced to the West, a strong desire for the smaller 10 lbs or less version of the Japanese Chin came to dominate and become the standard of various kennel clubs around the world.

Professor Ludvic von Schulmuth studied canine origins by studying the skeletal remains of dogs found in human settlements as long as the 8th millennium BC. The Professor created a genealogical tree of Tibetan dogs that shows the "Gobi Desert Kitchen Midden Dog", a scavenger, evolved into the "Small Soft-Coated Drop-Eared Hunting Dog". From this dog evolved the Tibetan Spaniel, Pekingese, and Japanese Chin`. Another branch coming down from the "Kitchen Midden Dog" gave rise to the Papillon and Long-haired Chihuahua and yet another "Kitchen Midden Dog" branch to the Pug and Shih Tzu.

Though there is some documentation that indicates Portuguese sailors introduced the breed to Europe in the 17th century by presenting some to Catherine of Braganza, Queen Consort to King Charles II of England, there is more credible evidence that the first Chin were gifted by the Emperor of Japan to an American naval officer, Matthew Calbraith Perry, when Perry visited the Orient in 1853 to open trade with the East. Perry was gifted with a total of seven (7) Chin; however, only two survived the passage back. Again, there is controversy over whether Perry gave the two to Franklin Pierce, President of the United States, gave them to James Stirling, Rear admiral of the Royal Navy to take to Queen Victoria, or gave them to his daughter, Caroline Slidell, after returning from Japan. Caroline was the wife of August Belmont.

Fictional Japanese Chin

- Himechin, from Fortune Dogs
- Ceaser, from the 2009 movie 2012 (film)

References

- Muszynski, Julie. *Henley: A New York Tail*. New York: Glitterati Incorporated, 2005. ISBN 1-57687-253-X

External links

- Japanese Chin Club of America [1]
- Japanese Chin breed information [2]
- Japanese Chin Club UK [3]
- Japanese Chin Care & Rescue Effort [4]

Maltese (dog)

The **Maltese** is a small breed of dog in the toy group, known for its silky white hair, though many owners of pet Maltese give them a short "puppy cut" for ease of grooming. The Maltese breed is descended from dogs originating in the Central Mediterranean Area. The breed name and origins are generally understood to derive from the Mediterranean island of Malta; however, the name is sometimes described with reference to the Adriatic island of Mljet, or a defunct Sicilian town called Melita.

History

This ancient breed has been known by a variety of names throughout the centuries. Originally called the "Canis Melitaeus" in Latin, it has also been known in English as the as the "ancient dog of Malta," the "Roman Ladies' Dog," the "Maltese Lion Dog," and the "Bichon" amongst other names. The Kennel Club settled on the name "Maltese" for the breed in the 19th century.

The Maltese is thought to have been descended from a Spitz type dog found among the Swiss Lake dwellers and was selectively bred to obtain its small size. There is also some evidence that the breed originated in Asia and is related to the Tibetan Terrier; however, the exact origin is unknown. The dogs probably made their way to Europe through the Middle East with the migration of nomadic tribes. Some writers believe these proto-Maltese were used for rodent control before the appearance of the breed gained paramount importance.

The oldest record of this breed was found on a Greek amphora found in the Etruscan town of Vulci, in which a Maltese-like dog is portrayed along with the word Μελιται (Melitaie). Archaeologists date this ancient Athenian product to the decades around 500 B. C. References to the dog can also be found in Ancient Greek and Roman literature.

Aristotle was the first to mention its name *Melitaei Catelli*, when he compares the dog to a Mustelidae, around 370 BC. The first written document (supported by Stephanus of Byzantium) describing the small *Canis Melitaeus* was given by the Greek writer Callimachus, around 350 BC. Pliny suggests the dog as having taken its name from the island of Adriatic island Méléda; however, Strabo, in the early first century AD, identifies the breed as originating from the Mediterranean island of Malta, and writes that they were favored by noble women.

During the first century, the Roman poet Martial wrote descriptive verses to a small white dog named Issa owned by his friend Publius. It is commonly thought that Issa was a Maltese dog, and various sources link Martial's Publius with the Roman Governor Publius of Malta, though others do not identify him.

John Caius, physician to Queen Elizabeth I, also claimed that Callimachus was referring to the island of Melita "in the Sicilian strait" (Malta). This claim is often repeated, especially by English writers. The dog's links to Malta are mentioned in the writings of Abbé Jean Quintin d'Autun, Secretary to the Grand Master of the Knights of Malta Philippe Villiers de L'Isle-Adam, in his work of 1536, *Insulae Melitae Descriptio.*

Around the 17th and 18th centuries some breeders decided to "improve" the breed, by making it smaller still. Linnaeus wrote in 1792 that these dogs were about the size of a squirrel. The breed nearly disappeared and was crossbred with other small dogs such as Poodles and miniature Spaniels. In the early 19th century there were as many as nine different breeds of Maltese dog.

Parti-colour and solid colour dogs were accepted in the show ring from 1902 until 1913 in England, and as late as 1950 in Victoria, Australia. However, white Maltese were required to be pure white. Coloured Maltese could be obtained from the south of France.

Description

The Maltese had been recognized as a FCI breed under the patronage of Italy in 1954, at the annual meeting in Interlaken, Switzerland. The current FCI standard is dated November 27, 1989, and the latest translation from Italian to English is dated April 6, 1998. The American Kennel Club recognized the breed in 1888, its latest standard being from March 10, 1964.

Appearance

Characteristics include slightly rounded skulls, with a finger-wide dome and black nose that is two finger-widths long. The body is compact with the length equaling the height. The drop ears with long hair and very dark eyes, surrounded by darker skin pigmentation (called a "halo"), gives Maltese their expressive look. Their noses can fade and become pink or light brown in color without exposure to sunlight. This is often referred to as a "winter nose" and many times will become black again with increased exposure to the sun.

Coat and color

The coat is long and silky and lacks an undercoat. The color is pure white; although cream or light lemon ears are permissible, they are not regarded as desirable. Also, a pale ivory tinge is permitted. In some standards, traces of pale orange shades are tolerated, but considered an imperfection.

Size

Adult Maltese range from roughly , though breed standards, as a whole, call for weights between . There are variations depending on which standard is being used. Many, like the American Kennel Club, call for a weight that is ideally less than 7 lb with between 4 and 6 lb preferred.

Temperament

Maltese are bred to be cuddly companion dogs, and thrive on love and attention. They are extremely lively and playful, and even as a Maltese ages, his or her energy level and playful demeanor remain fairly constant. Some Maltese may occasionally be snappish with smaller children and should be supervised when playing, although socializing them at a young age will reduce this habit. The Maltese is very active within a house, and, preferring enclosed spaces, does very well with small yards. For this reason, the breed also fares well in apartments and townhouses, and is a prized pet of urban dwellers. Maltese also suffer from separation anxiety, so potential owners should be cognizant of this behavior.

An Australia-wide (not including Tasmania) research project carried out in conjunction with RSPCA found owners likely to dump their Maltese terriers, citing the tendency of Maltese to bark constantly. This breed is Australia's most dumped dog.

Care

Maltese have no undercoat, and have little to no shedding if cared for properly. Like their relatives Poodles and Bichon Frisé, they are considered to be largely hypoallergenic and many people who are allergic to dogs may not be allergic to the Maltese (See list of Hypoallergenic dog breeds). Daily cleaning is required to prevent the risk of tear-staining.

Regular grooming is also required to prevent the coats of non-shedding dogs from matting. Many owners will keep their Maltese clipped in a "puppy cut," a 1 - 2" all over trim that makes the dog resemble a puppy. Some owners, especially those who show Maltese in the sport of conformation, prefer to wrap the long fur to keep it from matting and breaking off, and then to show the dog with the hair unwrapped combed out to its full length.

Dark staining in the hair around the eyes, "tear staining," can be a problem in this breed, and is mostly a function of how much the individual dog's eyes water and the size of the tear ducts. Tear stain can be readily removed if a fine-toothed metal comb, moistened with lukewarm water, is carefully drawn through the snout hair just below the eyes. This maintenance activity must be performed every two or three days, as a layer of sticky film is quick to redevelop. If the face is kept dry and cleaned daily, the staining can be minimized. Many veterinarians recommend avoiding foods treated with food coloring, and serving distilled water to reduce tear staining. There are also a few products on the market, for preventing tear stains.

Maltese are susceptible to "reverse sneezing," which sounds like a honking, snorting, or gagging sound and results often from overexcitement, play, allergies, or upon waking up. It's not life threatening, but owners should take measures to calm their Maltese down. Some owners cover the dog's nostrils to force it to breathe through its mouth. Always consult a physician if your Maltese reverse sneezes excessively.

Crossbred Maltese dogs

A crossbreed is a dog with two pure bred parents of different breeds. Dogs traditionally were crossed in this manner in hopes of creating a puppy with desirable qualities from each parent. Crossbreeds are typically larger than the pure breeds. For pet dogs, crosses may be done to enhance the marketability of puppies, and are often given portmanteau names. Maltese are often deliberately crossed with Shih Tzus and Poodles to produce small, fluffy lap dogs. Maltese-Poodle crosses are called Maltipoos. Maltese crossed with Pugs are also seeing an increase in popularity. Maltese with Shih Tzus are called *Mal-Shihs*, *Shihtese*, or *Mitzus*. This results in a dog which is a small, friendly animal and may have a unique low (or no) shedding coat.

Maltese crosses, like other crossbred dogs, are not eligible for registration by kennel clubs as they are not a *breed* of dog. Each kennel club has specific requirements for the registration of new breeds of dog, usually requiring careful record keeping for many generations, and the development of a breed club. At times, a crossbred dog will result in a new breed, as in the case in the 1950s when a Maltese and Lhasa Apso were accidentally bred. Descendants of that breeding are now a "purebred" breed of dog, the Kyi-Leo.

See also

- Bichon
- Lap dog
- Companion dog
- Companion Dog Group
- Toy Group

External links

- American Maltese Association [1]

Toy Manchester Terrier

The **Toy Manchester Terrier** is a breed of dog, categorized as a terrier. The breed was bred down in size in North America from the Manchester Terrier, and is placed in the Toy Group by the American Kennel Club and the Canadian Kennel Club (the Manchester Terrier is placed in the Terrier Group.) Neither the Fédération Cynologique Internationale nor the Kennel Club (UK) recognize a Toy variety of the Manchester Terrier.

History

The Manchester Terrier, from which the Toy Manchester Terrier was bred, was developed in the 1800s from crosses between an old Black and Tan Terrier with the Whippet, along with other breeds, primarily for rat-catching. In England, another breed was also developed in the 1800s in Manchester, the English Toy Terrier, as a separate breed from the Manchester Terrier. The English Toy Terrier was a popular pet in Victorian England, and bred to be very small, some weighing as little as 1 kg (2.2 lbs.)

The Toy Manchester Terrier breed was developed by breeding down the Manchester Terrier in size. In the United States in the 1920s the breed was called the Toy Black and Tan Terrier. The name was changed to the Toy Manchester Terrier and the American Toy Manchester Terrier Club was formed in the 1930s. The American Toy Manchester Terrier was recognised by the American Kennel Club in 1938, but by the 1950s the breed had declined and the breed club ceased to exist. Due to declining numbers of the breed, the Toy Manchester Terrier breed was re-defined as a size division of the Manchester Terrier in 1958 by the American Kennel Club, and the club name (including the two breeds as varieties) was changed to the American Manchester Terrier Club in 1958.

In England, the very similar English Toy Terrier (Black & Tan) has also declined, to the point where it is listed by the Kennel Club as being in danger of extinction. In order to rescue the breed, the Kennel Club has opened the stud book to allow certain selected examples of the North American Toy Manchester Terrier to be registered and bred as an English Toy Terrier (Black & Tan). However, the two breeds are not considered to be identical, and the standards for the two breeds show different requirements.

Appearance

The Toy Manchester Terrier in North America is a small, long legged dog with a short coat marked with tan, a long tail and ears which stand upright. In color and general conformation the Toy Manchester Terrier follows the standard for the Manchester Terrier. However, the Toy Manchester Terrier cannot exceed 12 pounds (5.4 kg) in weight; and, unlike the larger Manchester Terrier, for the Toy Manchester Terrier, cropped ears are a disqualification. Ears should be wide at the base and pointed at the tip. Flaring "bell" ears are a serious fault, meaning that it is undesireable to breed a dog with such ears; it does not mean that the dog has any disadvantages as a companion.

Black and Tan

Black and Tan is a dog coat colour that derives from one of the alleles known to exist at the genes mapped in dogs, and can be recognised with genetic testing (agouti gene, $a^t a^t$).

Similar breeds

The English Toy Terrier (Black and Tan) is considered to be the same breed as the Toy Manchester Terrier. In contrast with the Toy Manchester Terrier though, the desirable size for the English Toy Terrier (Black and Tan) is slightly smaller, and wider ears are also preferred.

The German Miniature Pinscher is another toy dog that some think resembles the Toy Manchester Terrier, but they really are quite different and have a very different ancestry.

The Russian Russkiy Toy is another similar dog, developed in Russia from early imports of the English Toy Terrier. They may be of various colours, not just Black and Tan, indicating a possible background in other breeds as well.

See also

- Toy Terrier
- Manchester Terrier
- English Toy Terrier (Black and Tan)
- Russkiy Toy

Miniature Pinscher

The **Miniature Pinscher** (**Zwergpinscher**, *Min Pin*) is a small breed of dog of the Pinscher type, developed in Germany. Miniature Pinschers were the first bred to hunt small mammals, especially rats. *Pinscher*, is a German word related to the English word "pincher", which is thought to refer to the ears of the breed which used to be 'pinched' or 'cropped'. *Zwerg* means *Dwarf*. The Miniature Pinscher is also known as the "King of the Toy Dogs". The international kennel club, the Fédération Cynologique Internationale, lists the Miniature Pinscher in Group 2, Section 1.1 *Pinscher*, along with the Dobermann, the German Pinscher, the Austrian Pinscher, and the other toy pinscher, the Affenpinscher. Other kennel clubs list the Miniature Pinscher in the Toy Group or Companion Group.

Description

Appearance

The original true Miniature Pinscher was more stout in appearance than today's refined dog. Its coat was more coarse and the dog in general was less refined. The refined look of today's dog was a result primarily of many who neglected to realize that the breed was a working breed and not a toy breed. Much of the natural look went away with years of breeding for the refined small dog now seen as today's Miniature Pinscher. Buyers should also be aware that there is no such dog as a "teacup" or "pocket" Min Pin: These are simply terms that certain breeders use to increase interest in their dogs (and sometimes the price).The miniature Pinscher also tends to have very long legs, and a small body, which can sometimes make it look quite comical. As a result of the flexible, agile body of a Miniature Pinscher, they are able to curl up in almost any position and almost always be comfortable.

Size

Miniature Pinscher breed standard calls for 10 to 12.5 inches at the withers (shoulders) with any dog under 10 or over 12.5 not eligible to be shown. The original Miniature Pinscher actually had more variance as being a cross between a smooth coated Dachshund and a Miniature Greyhound (known today as the Italian Greyhound, led to some carrying the Dachshund legs while others carried the Italian Greyhound leg creating some short and some tall. After many years of German breeding an average was maintained. Though today's standard is smaller than the original.

Coat and color

The coat is short and smooth, with colors, according to most breed standards, of red, stag-red, and black or chocolate with tan or rust markings, in addition to the blue and fawn. Blue coats, while admitted into the UK Kennel Club, can be registered in the American Kennel Club but cannot compete in show. They still benefit from all other aspects of the testicles AKC. The Miniature Pinscher frequently has a docked tail and cropped ears, though the AKC no longer requires ear cropping for shows. The AKC standard specifies a characteristic hackney-like action: "a high-stepping, reaching, free and easy gait in which the front leg moves straight forward and in front of the body and the foot bends at the wrist. The dog drives smoothly and strongly from the rear. The head and tail are carried high." The standard in Europe does not require the high stepping gait as the original Miniature Pinscher (zwergpinscher) did not walk in such a fashion. In Europe and Germany this high stepping gait is considered a fault.

The miniature pinscher will on occasion carry a small white patch generally located on neck or breast area. This links directly back to the original breed coloring. The Miniature Pinscher did come in Merle coloring which in the Dachshund is referred to as Dapple and in Harlequin like that found in the Great Dane. The white gene is part of the makeup of this breed; though breeders for years have fought to eliminate this gene, it is accepted by AKC in conformation and show so long as the area of white is limited to no more than 1/2 inch in direction.

Temperament

The miniature pinscher is an energetic dog that thrives on owner interaction. They are very loyal and are typically categorized as "one, or two person dogs", but with socialization, they can be integrated into families, and get along moderately with other dogs, pets, and children. Children, especially younger ones, must be encouraged to act gently to avoid being bit as these dogs are known to snap without any provocation. Teething can be one provocation. Socialization as puppies will help ensure they can co-exist and interact with other dogs as adults. Min Pins are known for biting people when being simply introduced as a stranger and are extremely protective of their owners. This protective instinct will manifest as nonstop barking and challenging postures. Although originally bred for ratting, they are also excellent watch dogs, barking at all things they deem a threat. These dogs can jump very high, some can jump five and a half feet in the air.

These little dogs will need lots of exercise per day. A backyard would be preferable so they can have an outdoor area to run around in, but it will need to be securely fenced in as this breed is the "Houdini" of the dog world when it comes to escaping.[1] The breed is a toy breed (AKC), these dogs' energy level exceeds the traditional concept or idea of the standard toy breed. Daily walks are not sufficient for this breed to wear off their excess energy. Though dog parks can be a solution, the true Miniature Pinscher, being a terrier, can go on the hunt at any moment, so an off-lead dog is a serious challenge with this breed. This dog truly does not see itself as small and therefore will challenge anything, including larger breeds. The breed is rated the 3rd worst breed for apartments due to overall lack of exercise as well as natural guarding instincts which lends the dog to barking and leads to many noise complaints. In addition, the dog can be quite destructive to homes and fixtures if the dog is not allowed ample time to expel its natural energy. Reports of damage to furniture, carpet, interior walls, doors, and other household products have been often reported. These dogs are only suitable for houses and apartments if they have regular exercise. A daily 45 minute+ exercise regimen is a must in order to have this dog in an apartment.

Care

- Miniature Pinschers that are not brought up with children may have a non-malicious problem with children; they can be yappy, but are actually being protective.

- Much care should be taken in educating youths about proper handling and play. The dogs are relatively sturdy for their size but can be easily injured by rough play with a child. In addition, their high-strung temperament leaves little patience for such rough play.

- Grooming is easy, as the smooth, short-haired coat requires little attention.

- As some Miniature Pinschers are prone to dry skin issues, bathing should be limited to no more than 3 to 4 times a year. During off periods a wipe down with a dampened towel should be used.

- In addition, care must be taken in colder weather as the coat provides virtually no protection from the cold.

- This also pertains to hot weather, with no guard hairs they can over heat.

- It is easier for them to be too cold than too hot, they usually do not like air conditioning that is set too low.

- Due to their instinct to hunt vermin, special care must be taken in preventing a Miniature Pinschers from "attacking" small objects, such as bottle caps, as they could pose a choking hazard.

- Miniature Pinschers are also prone to overeating and should have their diets monitored to prevent obesity. As with all dogs feeding them once a day to prevent any problems, though you may have to put a lot down; there should be food left over.

- This breed has an insatiable curiosity, so the best toys for Miniature Pinschers are ones that stimulate their curiosity. This may include toys that move or make an interesting noise. Miniature Pinschers enjoy having a collection of such toys, which they will hoard and spend much time in moving from one collecting place to another. However, Miniature Pinschers will chew and inevitably try to eat their toys, so avoid toys made of rubber or plastic. Small stuffed animals, rope toys, and interactive toys that pose a challenge work well. Cat toys (that do not have catnip) are also suitable. As with all dogs do not give them more than three toys at the same time as they will become possessive.

- Miniature Pinschers are territorial, so they should be provided with their own place to rest and sleep, though they will commonly stake a claim to a particular piece of furniture or curtain under or behind which they will sleep when people are in the room. They prefer to sleep on soft objects as well as under soft objects, so a small blanket should be provided so they can nestle. Unless the owner is amenable to sharing his or her bed, bedroom doors must be kept closed at night as Miniature Pinschers will jump onto beds and crawl under the covers. Care should be taken not to accidentally injure a Miniature Pinscher while they are sleeping under blankets. They can easily be trained to sleep on a soft object on the bed.

- It is essential due to the energy level of this breed that a secured fenced yard be provided; a bored Miniature Pinscher will become destructive. Miniature Pinschers need to exercise regularly. In addition, when in public this breed must be kept on harness and leash, as it is natural for this breed to give chase if something of interest catches its eye.
- Miniature Pinschers can make do with a medium sized yard, but daily walks are important, as is attention from their owners.
- Miniature Pinschers that have more than two puppies need help for the additional puppies to feed.

History

Although the Miniature Pinscher and the Doberman are similar in appearance, the Miniature Pinscher is not a "Miniature Doberman"; it predates the the Doberman by at least 50 years (although both are likely descended from the German Pinscher, but the relationship ends there). The Doberman Pinscher was bred by Karl Frederich Louis Dobermann in 1880, and Dobermann had noted that he was looking to create a dog resembling the Miniature "Zwergpinscher" Pinscher but 15 times larger.

In 1895, the Pinscher Schnauzer Klub officially recognized Dobermann's Pinscher. At that time they also officially recognized the Deutscher Pinscher (German Pinscher) as a separate breed from the Standard Schnauzer as well as the Reh Pinscher giving it the official name Zwergpinscher. The misconception in the U.S. that the Miniature Pinscher is a "miniature doberman" occurred because the Doberman Pinscher was introduced to the US before the Miniature Pinscher. In 1919 the Miniature Pinscher was introduced to the AKC show ring. At that time, not knowing that it was referred to officially in Germany as the Zwergpinscher (dwarfpinscher), the AKC referred to the breed as simply "Pinscher" and listed it in the miscellaneous category. By 1929 (the year of the breed's official introduction into the AKC), not noting it was a true *Terrier* breed, it was decided to officially place it in the *Toy* breed classification. Unfortunately the AKC's description, that the dog "must appear as a Doberman in miniature", led to the misconception common today that this breed is a "Miniature Doberman Pinscher". The original name for this breed in the US was "Pinscher" until 1972 when the name was officially changed to Miniature Pinscher.

The original Miniature Pinscher was not a true house pet but a working breed left to the barn with minimal human contact, much like feral cats on farms today. This may have contributed to the unique independent trait in the breed that is still found today.

Historical artifacts and paintings indicate that the Min Pin is a very old breed, but factual documentation begins less than 200 years ago, which leaves the breed's actual origins open to debate. In 1836 (the oldest documented writings on the breed history of the Miniature Pinscher) Dr. Reichenbach determined that the Miniature Pinscher was derived from crossing a smooth coated Dachshund (a favorite German breed of the time with excellent ratting skills) with an Italian

Greyhound. Additionally, many historians and those who have researched the background of the breed agree that the ancestry of the Miniature Pinscher most likely includes smaller German smooth-haired Pinschers, the Italian Greyhound and the Smooth Haired Dachshund. Including the Italian Greyhound made a swifter ratter as this breed was primarily used on farms where open fields required a faster dog to chase down rats and mice.

It must also be noted that the word "pinscher" in German does not translate to "terrier" as many believe but pinscher in German in fact translates to "biter". The word "terrier", like "setter", pertains to the way the breed works. The word "pinscher" is taken from the English word "pincher" to describe the biting action the breed uses when holding prey, pinching manner. As with all terriers, Miniature Pinschers were bred for the purpose of killing small animals, i.e. rats, mice etc.

See also

- Affenpinscher
- Companion dog
- Companion Dog Group
- Doxie-Pin
- Toy Group

External links

- American Kennel Club article on Miniature Pinschers [2], retrieved March 20, 2007.
- Miniature Pinscher Club of America [3]
- Canadian Miniature Pinscher Club [4]
- Internet Miniature Pinscher Service (IMPS), U.S. breed rescue organization [5]

Papillon (dog)

The **papillon** (from the French word for *butterfly*,), also called the Continental Toy Spaniel, is a breed of dog of the Spaniel type. One of the oldest of the toy Spaniels, it derives its name from its characteristic butterfly-like look of the long and fringed hair on the ears. A papillon with dropped ears is called a phalène (French for *moth*). The small head is slightly rounded between the ears with a well defined stop. The muzzle is somewhat short, thin tapering to the nose. The dark, medium sized, round eyes have thin black rims, often extending at the junction of the eyelids towards the ears. The large ears can either be erect or dropped with rounded tips. The teeth meet in a scissors bite. The long tail is set high carried over the body, and covered with long, fine hair. Dewclaws are sometimes removed. The straight, long, fine, single coat has extra frill on the chest, ears, back of the and the tail. Coat color is white with patches of any color. A mask of a color other than white covers both ears and eyes from back to front.

Description

Appearance

The papillon's ears are very large and butterfly-like. Papillons are parti-colored (white with markings of any color). An all white dog or a dog with no white is disqualified from the conformation show ring. A papillon without the signature white blaze extending down between the eyes is not disqualified.

Papillons can be registered with the American Kennel Club as the following colors, though not all of these colors are permitted in the conformation ring:

- White and Black
- White and Lemon
- White and Red
- White and Sable
- White Black and Tan
- Black Brown and White
- Black Red and White
- Brown and White
- Fawn and White
- Red
- Red White and Sable
- Sable
- White
- White and Liver

- White and Silver

The most distinctive aspect of the papillon is its large ears, which are well fringed with colored (not white) silky fur. The color covers both eyes and the front and back of the ears to give the ideal butterfly look. A white blaze and noseband is preferred over a solid-colored head. Nose, eye-rims, and lips should be black. Paw pads vary in color from black or pink depending on the coloring of the dog.

The papillon is considered to be a "wash and wear" breed and does not require excessive grooming. Papillons have a coat of fine fur, single length coat. As puppies, papillons have short length fur and as adults, the coat is long and silky. Their fur is very long, plush and soft to touch, until about three months old. It may take two years for a papillon to develop the tufts of hair that sprout off of its ears and chest.

There are two ear variations of this breed, the completely upright ears of the more common papillon, and the dropped spaniel-like ears of the Phalène. The American Kennel Club and the Fédération Cynologique Internationale consider the Phalène and the papillon the same breed. The papillon's coat is abundant, long, and silky. There is no undercoat. Ears are well-fringed with the inside covered with silken fur of medium length. Tail is long, well-fringed, set on high, arched over back with fringes falling to side to form plume. The head is slightly rounded between the ears, and the muzzle is fine, tapering, and narrower than the skull with an abrupt stop. Height: 20-28 cm (8-11 inches), over 11 inches is a fault and over 12 inches is a disqualification from the conformation show ring. Weight: 5-10 pounds (3–5 kg)

Temperament

The papillon has the appearance of a dainty toy breed, but many owners will claim that their dogs are "big dogs in little dog's body". Some people find that their papillon is very capable of handling a good five-mile walk. One aspect of the papillon that has led many to believe the "big dog" assertion is this breed's surprising athletic ability. In contrast to its staid and stately representation in the Old Master portraits, the papillon is highly energetic and intelligent. Provided their genetic structure is sound, and they are not the product of "puppy mill" inbreeding, they are generally healthy animals. Papillons are built for movement, and most do not need any encouragement to apply their energy to athletic activities. They enjoy at least a half hour running about. Papillons are considered a highly intelligent breed, often being ranked in the top ten dog breeds for intelligence.

Bred for centuries as lapdogs, a properly socialized papillon has a need to constantly be in the presence of its owner. Anywhere the owner goes, the papillon will be right behind. Because the dog will follow its owner from room to room, owners often find they have to look before they step, or they risk accidentally kicking the small dog. A papillon's agility, however, works to its advantage to prevent injuries: Once they have learned to be careful of where its owner steps, papillons have little trouble quickly moving out of the way. Their agility also means that they will leap on and off beds and couches several times their own height, presenting a risk of injury to their pencil-thin leg bones. Papillons will insist on sleeping directly next to their owners at night, and owners have to take care that they do not inadvertantly roll over on top of the dog, or push the dog over the side of the bed.

Papillons that are properly socialized and have not been abused welcome being handled by complete strangers, and owners may find difficulties keeping the dog away from visitors to their homes and strangers while on walks. They are social butterflies. Papillons are very playful by nature, and will welcome any chance to play with humans. However, care should be taken with the dog while around small children and toddlers who may unwittingly play too roughly and injure the dog in the process. Papillons can be highly protective of their owners, especially in the presence of larger dogs, but a well-socialized dog will not bite; under stress the papillon will instead bark loudly and excitedly run around.

Papillons have a reputation for being highly sensitive to their owner's moods. Owners may find that their papillon will act excited, start barking, or run and hide almost the instant the owner falls into a bad mood, even before any words are spoken. Papillons may recognize when their owner is about to leave them alone in the house, before the owner has reached for his keys or coat, and begin to whine or bark.

Activities

In recent years, the papillon has become a small dog star in the sport of dog agility. This sport consists of an obstacle course with tunnels, jumps, A-frames, and narrow bridges that a dog completes at top speed aided only by verbal and body-language commands from a handler. Agility requires the dog to spring, scramble, weave, and turn on a dime. The breed is considered naturally agile, and papillons compete at both national and international trials. Because many papillons have intense drive and natural speed, their tiny turning radius gives them an edge over larger dogs, and some papillons are capable of beating Border Collie speeds on some courses. At the same time, papillons excel in companionship and lap dog sweepstakes.

Others have experienced papillons as highly companionable—yet physically active—dogs requiring appropriate socialization, consistent and monitored exercise, continued training (which also serves to stimulate their active minds), and daily, proactive human-to-canine interaction.

History

The bistory of the papillon is traced through works of art. The earliest toy spaniels resembling the papillon are found in Italy. Tiziano Vicelli painted these small dogs in many famous paintings beginning around 1500 including the Venus of Urbino (1542). Other well known artists who included them in paintings are Watteau, Gonzalez Coques, Fragonard, Paolo Veronese, and Mignard. In a painting after Largillierre in the Wallace Collection in London, a papillon is clearly shown in a family portrait of Louis XIV. Papillons are also in paintings of royal families around Europe and paintings of merchant class families. The breed was popular in England, France, and Belgium, which are considered countries of origin by the FCI.

The "Titian spaniels" and those portrayed by later artists through Mignard and his contemporaries had the drooping ears characteristic of today's Phalène; it was not until the end of the 19th century that the erect-eared appearance became fashionable and gave the breed's modern name, papillon, French for "butterfly". The Titian spaniels were also exclusively red-and-white in coloration, in contrast to the many recognized colorations of today's papillon.

The papillon's history and long association with royalty have led to many stories about the breed. Marie Antoinette is said to have walked to the guillotine clutching her small dog under her arm, likely an apocryphal tale. However, tradition has it that Marie Antoinette's dog was a small spaniel that had been brought to the French court from Spain on the back of pack mules. According to the story, her pup was spared and cared for in a building in Paris still called the papillon House. Marie Antoinette's dog was said to have descended from a very old drop-eared breed known as the Epagneul Nain Continental, or *Continental Dwarf/Toy Spaniel* that appeared in church frescos and paintings as early as the 13th century.

The papillon is still officially referred to as the *Epagneul Nain Continental* (ENC) in non-English-speaking countries. The name *Squirrel Spaniel* also has been used, most likely referring to an earlier standard in which the tail set is described as "curling over the back as a squirrel's". One version of the history of the two varieties of ear shape in the ENC ("papillon" to denote the erect ear and "phalène" to denote the dropped ear) is that toward the end of the 19th century, breed fanciers bred a version of the spaniel whose ears stood up. This dog was said to have been nicknamed *papillon* based on the impressively large, erect ears that resembled the wings of a butterfly. The drop-eared variety of the breed came to be called the Phalène (which means "night moth"). Both types are still bred today and appear in the same litter. The papillon variety is much more common, although recently the Phalène has undergone a resurgence in popularity.

The papillon was first recognized by the AKC in 1935 with the formation of the Papillon Club of America. In 1999, Ch. Loteki Supernatural Being (call name "Kirby") owned and handled by John Oulton of Norwalk Connecticut, became the first papillon to win the prestigious "Best in Show" at the annual Westminster Kennel Club dog show. Kirby also won international success for the breed by taking the World Dog Show in Helsinki, Finland, and the Royal Invitational in Canada in 1998. Papillons also enjoy success today in competitive fields outside of conformation, including obedience and agility.

Famous Papillon owners

- Marie Antoinette owned a Phalène, the drop eared variety of papillons. All papillons were drop-eared until the 20th century.
- Madame de Pompadour and Henry III also had a Phalène, and possessed a very strong devotion to the breed.
- Actress Autumn Reeser of The O.C. owns a papillon named Gatsby after the book The Great Gatsby by F. Scott Fitzgerald.
- Tech expert Leo Laporte owns a papillon named Ozzy.
- George Takei, Mr. Sulu from Star Trek and official announcer of the Howard Stern Show on Sirius 100 owned a papillon named Reine (her full name is "La Reine Blanche" -- *The White Queen*).
- Porn star Ron Jeremy has two papillons, named Jenna and Tiffany. They can be seen in background of some of his movies.
- TV character Edna Birch from Emmerdale has a papillon named Tootsie.
- Legendary screen star Lauren Bacall never travels without her own well-behaved papillon.
- Singer Christina Aguilera owns two papillons, Chewy and Stinky.
- Artist Eliza Leahy owns a papillon, Gem, who is also a Psychiatric Service Dog
- Japanese pop singer Yuya Tegoshi has a papillon named Tiny.
- Magician and Juggler Dan Chan has a papillon named Ace who performs 200 shows a year with him
- Jane Kelly has two papillons called Trudy and Trixy.
- Musician Shinya Yamada owns a male papillon by the name of Ben (short for Benkei). Ben is depicted on a drum in one of Shinya's drum sets.
- Libertarian Radio Talk Show Host Neal Boortz owned a papillon named Coco.
- Jon Lajoie also owns a papillon by the name of Scruffy.
- Alex Gaskarth, vocalist of All Time Low owns a papillon named Sebastian.
- Sean Finney, author of the hit book The Travels of Mink, has a very hyper papillon named Rascal.
- Justin Bieber owns 1 papillon dog named Sammy
- George T. Mantzoros, Greek Billionaire owns a papillon named Jackie O'Nasty. She's a puppy.
- Sean Kennedy, vocalist of Tickle Me Pink owns two papillons named Jackie O and Norma Jean with his girlfriend Chelsea
- Patrick Halloran, lead singer of the Irish Rock band Ceann, has a papillon named Liam
- Jeremy McKinnon front man of A Day to Remember owns a Papillon named Timothy

See also

- Lap dog
- Companion dog
- Companion Dog Group
- Toy Group

Pekingese

The **Pekingese**, **Pekinese** or "**Peke**" (also commonly referred to as a "Lion Dog", or "Pelchie Dog" due to their resemblance to Chinese guardian lions) is an ancient breed of toy dog, originating in China. They were the favored pet of the Chinese Imperial court, and the name relates to the city of Beijing where the Forbidden City resides. The breed has several characteristics and health issues related to its unique appearance. Because of it's desirable characteristics, the Pekingese has been part of the development of other breeds, such as the Pekeatese.

Description

Appearance

The Pekingese breed is over 2000 years old and has hardly changed in all that time. One exception is that modern breeders and dog-show judges seem to prefer the long-haired type over the more-traditional spaniel-type coat.

The Pekingese's flat face is one of the breed's most obvious characteristics. The body is compact and low to the ground. Pekingese also have a muscular and durable body, which makes them great pets for small children as they can handle the accidental abuse that may come from being around small children. The legs are noticeably bowed and restrict the Pekingese's movement. The Peke's unusual rolling gait may have been deliberately bred to prevent the court dogs from wandering.

Coat

A Pekingese has a double coat. Trimming the coat is discouraged in show dogs. The Pekingese has a noticeable mane and feathering around the ears, tail and legs.

All breed standards allow all sorts of color combinations. The majority of Pekingese are gold, red or sable. Light gold, cream, black, white, sables, black and tan and occasionally 'blue' or slate grey have appeared in the breed. The latter often has poor pigment and light eyes. Albino Pekingese (white with pink eyes) should be bred cautiously due to health problems that have been associated with albinism.

A black mask or a self-colored face is equally acceptable in show dogs. Regardless of coat color the exposed skin of the muzzle, nose, lips and eye rims is black.

Size

Pekes weigh from and stand about at the withers, however they can sometimes be smaller. These smaller Pekes are commonly referred to as "Sleeve" Pekingese or just "Sleeves". The name is taken from ancient times, when emperors would carry the smallest of the breed in their sleeves. A Pekingese over 14 pounds is disqualified in the show ring.

The Pekingese is slightly longer than tall when measured from the forechest to the buttocks. The overall outline is an approximate ratio of 3 high to 5 long.

Health

The leading cause of death for Pekes, as for many other Toy breeds, is congestive heart failure. When diagnosed early and successfully treated with medication, a Peke with this problem can expect to live many years. A heart murmur is a potential sign of a problem, and must be evaluated by a veterinary cardiologist. Very often, the problem does not surface until the dog is 6 or more years old, so it is very difficult to screen the problem in a pup.

Pekes' other main problems are eye issues and breathing problems, resulting from its tiny skull and flattened face, and skin allergies (and hotspots). An especially common problem is eye ulcers, which may develop spontaneously. Pekes should never be kept outside as their flattened faces and noses can develop breathing problems, which makes it difficult for them to regulate their body temperature in overly hot or cold weather. Their long backs, relative to their legs, make them vulnerable to back injuries. Care should be taken, when picking them up, to give Pekes adequate back support: one hand under the chest, the other under the abdomen. Short legs give some Pekes difficulty with stairs; older dogs may not be able to go up or down stairs alone.

In an effort to address the breathing difficulties caused by the Peke's flat face, the Kennel Club (UK) significantly changed the breed standard in October 2008, removing the clause that the "profile [should be] flat with nose well up between eyes" and adding instead that the "muzzle must be evident". This was in response to public opinion following the BBC programme, Pedigree Dogs Exposed. The breed standards of two other flat faced breeds, the Pug and English Bulldog, were soon also changed.

Care

Keeping the Peke coat healthy and presentable requires daily brushing if it is an outside dog. If you do this, they will need to see a groomer only once every 3 months. If a Peke becomes dirty, it is important to take it to a groomer as soon as possible, as it is difficult to remove dirt from its coat once it has dried, but this can be avoided by brushing regularly, especially the belly, and between the front and hind legs. One important thing for new owners to remember is that dogs intended as a house pet may be kept in a puppy cut which is much more low maintenance than a show cut. It is also important to remove dirt from the eye pores daily, and from the creases on the face to prevent sores (hotspots).

Due to their abundance of fur, it is important to keep the Pekingese cool. Pekes are indoor dogs and they are prone to having heatstroke when exposed to high temperature.

History

The breed originated in China in antiquity, in the city of Peking. Recent DNA analysis confirms that the Pekingese breed is one of the oldest breeds of dog, one of the least genetically diverged from the wolf. For centuries, they could be owned only by members of the Chinese Imperial Palace.

During the Second Opium War, in 1860, the Forbidden City was occupied by a contingent of British and French troops. The Emperor Xianfeng had fled with all of his court to Chengde. However, an elderly aunt of the emperor remained. When the 'foreign devils' (Europeans) entered, she committed suicide. She was found with her five Pekingese mourning her passing. They were removed by the Allies before the palace was burnt to the ground.

Lord John Hay took a pair, later called '*Schloff*', and '*Hytien*' and gave them to his sister, the Duchess of Wellington, wife of Henry Wellesley, 3rd Duke of Wellington. Sir George Fitzroy took another pair, and gave them to his cousins, the Duke and Duchess of Richmond and Gordon. Lieutenant Dunne presented the fifth Pekingese to Queen Victoria of the United Kingdom, who named it *Looty*.

The Empress Dowager Cixi presented Pekingese to several Americans, including John Pierpont Morgan and Alice Lee Roosevelt Longworth, daughter of Theodore Roosevelt, who named it *Manchu*. The first Pekingese in Ireland was introduced by Dr. Heuston. He established smallpox vaccination clinics in China. The effect was dramatic. In gratitude, the Chinese minister, Li Hung Chang presented him with a pair of Pekingese. They were named *Chang* and *Lady Li*. Dr. Heuston founded the Greystones kennel.

Around the turn of the century, Pekingese dogs became popular in Western countries. They were owned by such arbiters of fashion as Queen Alexandra of the United Kingdom, and Elsie de Wolfe, popular American interior decorator.

Sleeve Pekingese

According to the 1948 publication *Dogs In Britain, A Description of All Native Breeds and Most Foreign Breeds in Britain* by Clifford LB Hubbard, the Sleeve Pekingese is a true miniature of the standard-sized dog, and was also known as the Miniature Pekingese. The name *Sleeve Pekingese* came from the custom of carrying these small dogs in the capacious sleeves of the robes worn by members of the Chinese Imperial Household. Hubbard indicated that this tradition appeared to be early Italian rather than Chinese, but its adoption by the Chinese Imperial Household led to dogs being bred as small as possible and to practices aimed at stunting their growth: giving puppies rice wine, holding new-borns tightly for hours at a time or putting the puppies into tight-fitting wire mesh waistcoats. These practices were apparently forbidden by the late Dowager Empress Tzu Hsi.

In Hubbard's time, the term *Sleeve* was applied in Britain to a miniature Pekingese no more than 6-7 pounds in weight, often appearing to be only about 3-4 pounds. Mrs Flander's *Mai Mai* weighed only a little over 4 pounds and many other breeders had bred true miniatures of a similar size. He noted that miniatures may appear in a litter bred from full-sized Pekingese and were exhibited in classes for dogs less than 7 pounds at the major dog shows in Britain. In 1946 (when Hubbard wrote his book), the Sleeve Pekingese had a strong following with the most popular colours being cream and white, with white being considered particularly attractive. He illustrated the description with a white Sleeve Pekingese bred by Mrs Aileen Adam.

Quotation

Her Imperial Majesty, Empress Dowager Cixi, said:

Let the Lion Dog be small; let it wear the swelling cape of dignity around its neck; let it display the billowing standard of pomp above its back.

Let its face be black; let its forefront be shaggy; let its forehead be straight and low.

Let its eyes be large and luminous; let its ears be set like the sails of war junk; let its nose be like that of the monkey god of the Hindus.

Let its forelegs be bent; so that it shall not desire to wander far, or leave the Imperial precincts.

Let its body be shaped like that of a hunting lion spying for its prey.

Let its feet be tufted with plentiful hair that its footfall may be soundless and for its standard of pomp let it rival the whick of the Tibetans' yak, which is flourished to protect the imperial litter from flying insects.

Let it be lively that it may afford entertainment by its gambols; let it be timid that it may not involve itself in danger; let it be domestic in its habits that it may live in amity with the other beasts, fishes or birds that find protection in the Imperial Palace.

And for its color, let it be that of the lion - a golden sable, to be carried in the sleeve of a yellow robe; or the colour of a red bear, or a black and white bear, or striped like a dragon, so that there may be dogs appropriate to every costume in the Imperial wardrobe.

Let it venerate its ancestors and deposit offerings in the canine cemetery of the Forbidden City on each new moon.

Let it comport itself with dignity; let it learn to bite the foreign devils instantly.

Let it be dainty in its food so that it shall be known as an Imperial dog by its fastidiousness; sharks fins and curlew livers and the breasts of quails, on these may it be fed; and for drink give it the tea that is brewed from the spring buds of the shrub that groweth in the province of Hankow, or the milk of the antelopes that pasture in the Imperial parks.

Thus shall it preserve its integrity and self-respect; and for the day of sickness let it be anointed with the clarified fat of the legs of a sacred leopard, and give it to drink a throstle's eggshell full of the juice of the custard apple in which has been dissolved three pinches of shredded rhinoceros horn, and apply it to piebald leeches.

So shall it remain - but if it dies, remember thou too art mortal.

Peke legends

There are two origin stories for the Pekingese. The first is the most common, The Lion and the Marmoset:

A lion and a marmoset fell in love. But the lion was too large. The lion went to the Buddha and told him of his woes. The Buddha allowed the lion to shrink down to the size of the marmoset. And the Pekingese was the result.

The second, less-common, originating story is The Butterfly Lions:

A lion fell in love with a butterfly. But the butterfly and lion knew the difference in size was too much to overcome. Together they went to see the Buddha, who allowed their size to meet in the middle. From this, the Pekingese came.

Another legend says that the Peke resulted from the mating of a lion and a monkey, getting its nobleness and coat from the former and its ungainly walk from the latter.

Because the Pekingese was believed to have originated from the Buddha, he was a temple dog. As such, he was not a mere toy. He was made small so that he could go after and destroy little demons that might infest the palace or temple. But his heart was big so that he could destroy even the largest and fiercest. (Barbara Hambly's novel, *Bride of the Rat God*, was written from this premise, although Hambly denies knowledge of the legends.)

Famous Pekes

- Bambi, pet of Miss Marjory Warner, upon whom James Herriot based his characters **Mrs. Pumphrey** and **Tricki Woo**
- Chu-Chu from The Amazing Chan and the Chan Clan
- Fifi the Peke, the girlfriend of Pluto, Mickey Mouse's pet.
- Buster, Pet of Chinese folk historian Onoj Ewalg
- Manchu, pet of Theodore Roosevelt's daughter, Alice Lee Roosevelt Longworth.
- Winnie/Wednesday, pet of Bridget Marquardt, Hugh Hefner's girlfriend, as seen on E!'s *The Girls Next Door*.
- Sun Yat owned by Henry Sleeper Harper - Harper Brothers Publishing - was a survivor on the .
- Penelope, pet of Philadelphia composer Joseph Hallman
- The three pekes from Sagwa, the Chinese Siamese Cat

- Harm, the black peke from the Barker and Llewelyn Victorian mystery series by Will Thomas

See also

- Foo Dog, dog breeds originating in China that resemble Chinese guardian lions and hence are also called Foo or Fu Dogs or Lion Dogs.

Pomeranian (dog)

The **Pomeranian** (often known as a **Pom**, or more humorously, **Pom Pom**) is a breed of dog of the Spitz type, named for the Pomerania region in Central Europe (today part of eastern Germany and northern Poland). Classed as a toy dog breed because of its small size, the pomerianian is descended from the larger Spitz type dogs, specifically the German Spitz. It has been determined by the Fédération Cynologique Internationale to be part of the German Spitz breed, and in many countries, they are known as the **Zwergspitz** (*Dwarf Spitz*), or **Toy German Spitz**.

The breed was made popular by a number of royal owners during the 17th and 18th centuries. Queen Victoria owned a particularly small Pomeranian at the time, and consequently the smaller variety became universally popular. During Queen Victoria's lifetime alone, the size of the breed decreased by 50%. Pomeranians respond well to firm, consistent obedience training, but otherwise will do what they please. They are known to bark defensively in response to any outside noise. Overall the pomeranian is a sturdy, healthy dog. The most common health issue is Luxating patella. Tracheal collapse can also be an issue. More rarely, they can suffer from a skin condition colloquially known as "black skin disease", or alopecia ex. This is a genetic disease which causes the dogs skin to turn black and lose all or most of its hair. The breed is currently among the top 15 most popular in the USA, and the current fashion for small dogs has increased their popularity worldwide. While they are very small dogs, they are sometimes protective of their owners. Their size can also make them nip if surprised.

Description

Appearance

Pomeranians are small dogs weighing and standing high at the withers. They are compact but sturdy dogs with an abundant textured coat with a highly plumed tail set high and flat. The top coat forms a ruff of hair on the neck and back, and they also have a fringe of feathery hair on the hindquarters.

The earliest Poms were white or occasionally black, however Queen Victoria adopted a small red Pomeranian in 1888, which caused that color to become fashionable by the end of the 19th century. In modern times, the Pomeranian comes in the widest variety of colors of any dog breed, including white, black, brown, red, orange, cream, blue, sable, black and tan, brown and tan, spotted, brindle, plus combinations of those colors. The most common colors are orange, black or cream/white.

The merle pomeranian is a recent color developed by breeders. It is a combination of a solid base color with lighter blue/grey patch which gives a mottled effect. The most common base colors for the effect are red/brown or black, although it can also appear with other colors. Combinations such as brindle merle or liver merle are not accepted in the breed standard. In addition, the eye, nose and paw pad colors are different in merles, changing parts of the eye to blue and the color on the nose and paw pads to become mottled pink and black.

Pomeranians have a thick double coat, and while grooming is not difficult, breeders recommend that it is done daily because of the thickness of the coat and the constant shedding. The outer coat is long straight, and harsh in texture while the undercoat is soft, thick and short. The coat knots and tangles easily, particularly when the undercoat is being shed, which happens twice a year.

Behavior

Pomeranians are typically a very friendly and lively breed of dog. They love to be around their owners and are known to be protective of them as well. They bond quickly with their owners, and can suffer from separation anxiety if not trained to spend time alone. Pomeranians are alert and aware of changes in their environment and barking at new stimuli can develop into a habit of barking excessively in any situation. They are somewhat defensive of their territory and will thus bark when they encounter any outside noises. Pomeranians are intelligent dogs, respond well to training, and can be very successful in getting what they want from their owners.

They tend to seek out cooler environments, and it is common to find one lying down on a cold floor like a tiled floor that is usually cold in the night and day. The breed is good for apartment living, and are very active indoors.

Health

Overall health

The average life expectancy of a Pomeranian is 12 to 16 years. A well bred dog on a good diet with appropriate exercise will have few health problems, and if kept trim and fit a Pomeranian is a sturdy little dog. The breed does have similar health issues to many dog breeds, although some issues such as hip dysplasia are not common due to the Pomeranian's lightweight build. Some health issues can develop as a result of lack of attention to grooming, and teeth, ear and eye cleaning. However, with routine care these problems can be avoided.

Common problems

Merle colored dogs may suffer from mild to severe deafness, increased intraocular pressure, ametropia, microphthalmia and colobomas. Merle dogs born from parents who are also both merles may additionally suffer from abnormalities of the skeletal, cardiac and reproductive systems.

Luxating patellas is the most common health issue in the Pomeranian breed. It occurs when through either malformation or trauma, the ridges forming the patellar grove in the knee are not prominent and are too shallow to allow the patella to properly sit securely. This can cause the patella to "luxate" (jump out of the grove) sideways which will cause the leg to lock up with the foot off the ground. Whilst the muscles are contracted the patella cannot return to the correct position. The initial pain is caused by the knee cap sliding across the ridges of the femur. Once out of position, the dog does not feel any pain caused by the slipped disc. This condition is more common among the smaller breeds, especially the Miniature and Toy Poodles.

Tracheal collapse is caused by a weakening of the tracheal rings in the windpipe. It occurs when the rings that normally hold the shape of the windpipe collapse, closing the airway. It is commonly seen in Pomeranians and other small breed dogs such as Yorkshire Terriers and Poodles. The symptoms of a collapse include a honking cough that can sound similar to a Goose honk, an intolerance to exercise, fainting spells and a cough that is worsened by hot weather, exercise and excitement.

In Pomeranians, a condition often called "black skin disease" occurs which is a combination of alopecia (hair loss) and hyperpigmentation (a darkening of the skin). Other names for this condition include wooly coat, coat funk, pseudo-Cushing's disease, or severe hair loss syndrome. This condition affects male Pomeranians more than females, and may be inherited. Several other breeds have this same skin disorder including the American Water Spaniel, Dachshund, Keeshond and Chow Chow. Although most affected dogs show signs following puberty, it can occur at any age. Other conditions can mimic this condition including Cushing's syndrome, hypothyroidism, chronic skin infections, and reproductive hormone disorders.

Another common disorder in male Pomeranians is cryptorchidism. This is when either one or both of the testicles do not descend. In this case surgery is needed to cut into their abdomen to remove them. The good news is that it makes them healthier and reduces risk of cancer following other problems.

History

Origins

The forerunners of today's Pomeranian breed were large working dogs from the Arctic regions. These dogs are commonly known as the Wolfspitz or Spitz type, which is German for "sharp point" which was the term originally used by Count Eberhard zu Sayn in the 16th Century as a reference to the features of the dog's nose and muzzle. The Pomeranian is considered to be descended from the German

Spitz.

The breed is thought to have acquired its name by association with the area which is now the northeast region of Germany, known as Pomerania. Although not the origin of the breed, this area is credited with the breeding which led to the original Pomeranian type of dog. However, proper documentation was lacking until the pomeranian's introduction into the United Kingdom.

An early modern recorded reference to the Pomeranian breed is from 2 November 1764, in a diary entry in James Boswell's *Boswell on the Grand Tour: Germany and Switzerland*. "The Frenchman had a Pomeranian dog named Pomer whom he was mighty fond of." The offspring of a Pomeranian and a wolf bred by an animal merchant from London is discussed in Thomas Pennant's *A Tour in Scotland* from 1769.

Two members of the British Royal Family influenced the evolution of the breed. In 1767, Queen Charlotte, Queen-consort of King George III of England, brought two Pomeranians to England. Named Phoebe and Mercury, the dogs were depicted in paintings by Sir Thomas Gainsborough. These paintings depicted a dog larger than the modern breed, reportedly weighing as much as , but showing modern traits such as the heavy coat, ears and a tail curled over the back.

Queen Victoria, Queen Charlotte's granddaughter, was also an enthusiast and established a large breeding kennel. One of her favoured dogs was a comparatively small red sable Pomeranian which she named "Windor's Marco" and was reported to weigh only . When she first exhibited Marco in 1891, it caused the smaller type Pomeranian to become immediately popular and breeders began selecting only the smaller specimens for breeding. During her lifetime, the size of the Pomeranian breed was reported to have decreased by 50%. Queen Victoria worked to improve and promote the Pomeranian breed by importing smaller Pomeranians of different colors from various European countries to add to her breeding program. Royal owners during this period also included Joséphine de Beauharnais, wife of Napoleon I of France and King George IV of England.

The first breed club was set up in England in 1891, and the first breed standard was written shortly afterwards. The first member of the breed was registered in America to the American Kennel Club in 1898, and it was recognised soon afterwards in 1900. Glen Rose Flashaway won the Toy Group at the Westminster Kennel Club Dog Show in 1926, the first Pomeranian to win a group at Westminster. It would take until 1988 for the first Best in Show at Westminster, Great Elms Prince Charming II.

In the standard published in 1998, the Pomeranian is included in the German Spitz standard, along with the Keeshond, by the Fédération Cynologique Internationale. According to the standard "Spitz breeds are captivating" and have a "unique characteristic, cheeky appearance."

Popularity

The Pomeranian has been among the more popular dog breeds in the United States, consistently in the top 15 of registered AKC dog breeds over the last 10 years. The breed ranked #13 in the 2008 rankings having attained the same ranking in 2007 and 2003.

However, it is not listed in the top 20 breeds in the UK in either 2007 or 2008. In Australia their popularity has declined since 1986, with a peak of 1128 Pomeranians registered with the Australian National Kennel Council in 1987, however only 577 were registered in 2008. But this itself is an increase from 2004, when only 491 dogs were registered.

It is more popular in American cities in 2008, ranking joint tenth (with American Bulldog) in Detroit and Orlando, ninth in Los Angeles, a joint seventh in Seattle (again, with the American Bulldog), but third in Honolulu, only bested by the Labrador Retriever and the German Shepherd Dog.

See also

- Lap dog
- Companion dog
- Companion Dog Group

Poodle

For the political insult see poodle (insult).

The **poodle** is a breed of dog, and is regarded as the second most intelligent breed of dog after the border collie, and before the German Shepherd. The poodle breed is found officially in toy, miniature, and standard sizes, with many coat colors. Originally bred as a type of water dog, the poodle is skillful in many dog sports, including agility, obedience, tracking, and even herding. Poodles are elegant in the conformation ring, having taken top honors in many shows, including "Best in Show" at the Westminster Kennel Club Dog Show in 1991 and 2002, and at the World Dog Show in 2007.

History

Poodles are retrievers or gun dogs, and can still be seen in that role. The poodle is believed to have originated in Germany, where it is known as the Pudel. The English word "poodle" comes from the Low German *pudel* or *puddeln* , meaning to splash in the water. The breed was standardized in France, where it was commonly used as a water retriever.

The American Kennel Club states that the large, or Standard, Poodle is the oldest of the three varieties and that the dog gained special fame as a water worker. So widely was it used as retriever that it was bred with a moisture-resistant coat to further facilitate progress in swimming. Thence came the custom of clipping to pattern which so enhanced the style and general appearance that its sponsors, particularly in France, were captivated by it. All of the Poodle's ancestors were acknowledged to be good swimmers, although one member of the family, the truffle dog (which may have been of Toy or Miniature size), it is said, never went near the water. Truffle hunting was widely practiced in England, and later in Spain and Germany, where the edible fungus has always been considered a delicacy. For scenting and digging up the fungus, the smaller dogs were favored, since they did less damage to the truffles with their feet than the larger kinds. So it is rumored that a terrier was crossed with the Poodle to produce the ideal truffle hunter.

Despite the standard poodle's claim to greater age than the other varieties, there is some evidence to show that the smaller types developed only a short time after the breed assumed the general type by which it is recognized today. The smallest, or Toy variety, was developed in England in the 18th century, when the White Cuban became popular there. This was a sleeve dog attributed to the West Indies from whence it traveled to Spain and then to England. The continent had known the poodle long before it came to England. Drawings by the German artist, Albrecht Durer, establish the breed in the 15th and 16th centuries. It was the principal pet dog of the later 18th century in Spain, as shown by the paintings of the Spanish artist Francisco Goya. France had toy poodles as pampered favorites during the reign of Louis XVI at about the same period.

Characteristics

Appearance

Most poodles have a dense, curly, non-sheddingcoat that requires regular grooming. Since poodles do not have the plush double coat of many breeds, their fur is often referred to as "hair", a term usually reserved for humans. Most poodles are solid-colored, and many registries allow only solid colors in conformation shows. "Parti" (short for parti-colored) poodles have large patches of colors different from the main body color. "Phantom" poodles have the color pattern of a black-and-tan dog, although not necessarily black and tan. Solid-colored poodles may either "hold" their color (i.e., stay more or less the same throughout their lives) or "fade" or "clear" to a lighter shade. Usually the ears and the thicker guard hairs hold more of the original color than other hair.

The tail is usually poofy, often docked in the US and less often in Europe; the practice is illegal in the UK and Australia. Tails, when docked, are left much longer than in the past. "Bunny-like tails" (very short-docked tails) are now rarely seen except among puppy mill pet shop dogs. Poodles have drop ears which are never cropped.

Poodle sizes

Unlike many breeds, poodles can come in a variety of sizes, distinguished by adult shoulder (withers) height. The exact height cutoffs among the varieties vary slightly from country to country. Non-Fédération Cynologique Internationale kennel clubs generally recognize three sizes, *standard*, *miniature*, and *toy*, sometimes as sizes of the same breed, and sometimes as separate breeds. The Fédération Cynologique Internationale recognizes four sizes of one breed, *standard*, *medium*, *miniature*, and *toy*. Only the Fédération Cynologique Internationale describes a maximum size for standard poodles. France is the country responsible for the breed in the Fédération Cynologique Internationale, and in this country the puppies of all sizes are listed together.. The terms *royal standard*, *teacup*, and *tiny teacup* are marketing names, and are not recognized by any major kennel club.

Comparison of poodle sizes defined by major kennel clubs

Size	The Kennel Club (UK)	Australian National Kennel Council	New Zealand Kennel Club	Canadian Kennel Club	American Kennel Club	United Kennel Club	Fédération Cynologique Internationale
Standard, Grande	over 38 cm (15 ins)	38 cm (15 ins) and over	38 cm (15 ins) and over	over 15 inches (38 cm)	over 15 inches (38 cm)	over 15 inches (38 cm)	over 45 cm to 60 cm (+2 cm) (18ins to 24ins)
Medium, Moyen	not used	not used	not used	not used	not used	not used	over 35 cm to 45 cm (14ins to 18ins)
Miniature - Dwarf, Nain	28 cm to 38 cm (11ins to 15ins)	28 cm to under 38 cm (11ins to 15ins)	28 cm to under 38 cm (11ins to 15ins)	over 10ins to under 15ins (25.4 cm to 38 cm)	over 10ins to 15ins (25.4 cm to 38 cm)	over 10ins up to 15ins (25.4 cm to 38 cm)	over 28 cm to 35 cm (11ins to 14ins)
Toy	under 28 cm (11 ins)	under 28 cm (11 ins)	under 28 cm (11 ins)	under 10ins (25.4 cm)	under 10ins (25.4 cm)	under 10ins (25.4 cm)	24 cm to 28 cm (9.4ins to 11ins)

All the Fédération Cynologique Internationale poodles are in Group 9 *Companion and Toy*, Section 2 *Poodle*. All the Kennel Club poodles are in the Utility Group. All three sizes of poodle for the Australian National Kennel Council and the New Zealand Kennel Club are in the Non-Sporting Group. The Canadian Kennel Club and the American Kennel Club place standard and miniature sizes in the Non-Sporting Group, and the toy size in the Toy Group. The United Kennel Club places the miniature and toy in the Companion Group and the standard poodle in the Gundog Group.

Coat

Unlike most dogs which have double coats, poodles have a single layer (no undercoat) of dense, curly fur that sheds minimally and could be considered hypoallergenic (though not completely allergen free). Texture ranges from coarse and woolly to soft and wavy. Poodle show clips require many hours of brushing and care per week, about 10 hours/week for a standard poodle. Poodles are usually clipped down as soon as their show career is over and put into a lower-maintenance cut. Pet clips are much less elaborate than show and require much less maintenance. A pet owner can anticipate grooming a poodle every six to eight weeks. Although professional grooming is often costly, poodles are easy to groom at home with the proper equipment.

Show clips

Many breed registries allow only certain clips for poodles shown in conformation. In American Kennel Club shows, adults must be shown in the "Continental" or "English saddle" clips. Dogs under 12 months old may be shown with a "puppy clip." The United Kennel Club (US) allows in addition a *Sporting Clip*, similar to the puppy clip, with the fur trimmed short for hunting dogs. The American Kennel Club allows the Sporting Clip in Stud Dog and Brood Bitch classes as well.

Some sources believe the show clips evolved from working clips, which originally provided warmth to major joints when the dogs were immersed in cold water. The rest of the body is shaved for less drag in the water. Others express skepticism at this theory, instead citing the French circus as the origin of the entertaining and unique clips.

Second Puppy

This clip is also called the Scandinavian clip or puppy clip. It was invented by Swedish and Norwegian show groomers in the 1970s. This clip is the most common one in all sizes for shows in Europe, and is allowed for adult poodles to be shown in the FCI countries. The face, throat, belly, feet and the base of the tail are shaved 5 to 7 days before the show to get a nice smooth appearance of the shaved areas. The hair on the head is left to form a "topknot" that is fixed by using latex bands; in most European countries, hair spray is banned. The rest of the dog is shaped with scissors. It makes the parts of the dog look fluffy.

Continental clip

In the continental clip the face, throat, feet and part of the tail are shaved. The upper half of the front legs is shaved, leaving "fluffy pompons" around the ankles. The hindquarters are shaved except for pompons on the lower leg (from the hock to the base of the foot) and optional round areas (sometimes called "rosettes") over the hips. The continental clip is the most popular show clip today.

English Saddle clip

The English saddle clip is similar to the continental, except for the hindquarters. The hindquarters are not shaved except a small curved area on each flank (just behind the body), the feet, and bands just below the stifle (knee) and above the hock, leaving three pompons. This clip is now rarely seen in standard poodles.

Pet clips

Pet clips can be simple or as elaborate as owners wish. The hair under the tail should always be kept short to keep feces from matting in the poodle's curls. Most owners also keep the feet and face clipped short to prevent dirt from matting between toes and food from matting around the dog's muzzle. Beyond these sanitary requirements, desired clips depend on owners' preferences. Some owners maintain a longer clip in winter than summer, which they groom often with a wire slicker brush to remove tangles and prevent matting.

Corded coat

In most cases, whether a poodle is in a pet or show clip, hair is completely brushed out. Poodle hair can also be "corded" with rope-like mats similar to those of a Komondor or human dreadlocks. Though once as common as the curly poodle, corded poodles are now rare. Corded coats are difficult to keep clean and take a long time to dry after washing. Any poodle with a normal coat can be corded when their adult coat is in. Corded poodles may be shown in all major kennel club shows.

Temperament

Otherwise notable is this breed's keen sense for instinctual behavior. In particular, marking and hunting drives are more readily observable than in most other breeds. Even Toys will point birds. Classified as highly energetic, poodles can also get bored fairly easily and have been known to get creative about finding mischief. Poodles like to be in the center of things and are easily trained to do astonishing tricks involving both brains and agility. They have performed in circuses for centuries, beginning in Europe, and have been part of the Ringling Circus in its various forms from its inception. The Grimaldis, the famous British clowns Kenneth and Audrey Austin, "developed a stronger circus act" with a clever poodle named 'Twinkle,' the success of which allowed them to continue performing even as octogenarians."

Poodles are extremely people-oriented dogs and generally eager to please. Standard poodles in particular tend to be good with children. Poodles are adaptable and easy to train. Like most dogs, they appreciate daily exercise, such as a walk or a play session. Most are fairly agile and athletic.

Toy poodles will play ball and love to fetch. Play time is vital, but one must be sure that they get plenty of rest following long play periods and that fresh water is available at all times.

Poodles are very easy to housebreak. Whether going outside or being trained on a pad, they learn quickly where to defecate. They are still animals, however, and they need time to understand what is desired of them. It may take a while, but poodles are quite smart and learn more quickly than most dogs.

Health

The most common serious health issues of standard poodles (listed in order of the number of reported cases in the Poodle Health Registry [1] (as of August 20, 2007) are Addison's disease, gastric dilatation volvulus (GDV = bloat/torsion), thyroid issues (hyperthyroid and hypothyroid), tracheal collapse, epilepsy, sebaceous adenitis, juvenile renal disease, hip dysplasia, and cancer. Standard poodles are also susceptible to some health issues usually too minor to report to the poodle health registry. The most common of these minor issues are probably ear infections. Ear infections are a problem in all poodle varieties. Ear problems can be minimized by proper ear care. A veterinarian should be consulted if the dog shows signs of an ear infection.

Addison's Disease

Addison's disease is (as of August 20, 2007) the illness most commonly reported to the Poodle Health Registry. The number of reported cases of Addison's disease is nearly twice as high as the next most common problem (GDV). Addison's disease is characterized by insufficient production of glucocorticoid and/or mineralocortoid in the adrenal cortex. Addison's is often undiagnosed because early symptoms are vague and easily mistaken for other conditions. Standard poodles with unexplained lethargy, frequent gastric disturbances, or an inability to tolerate stress should be tested for Addison's. Addison's can cause fatal sodium/potassium imbalances, but, if caught early and treated with lifelong medication, most dogs can live a relatively normal life.

Gastric dilatation volvulus

Standard poodle owners should take special note of the high incidence of GDV in this breed. Excess gas trapped in the dog's stomach causes "bloat." Twisting of the stomach (volvulus or "torsion") causes or is caused by excess gas. Symptoms include restlessness, inability to get comfortable, pacing, or retching without being able to bring up anything. The dog's abdomen may be visibly swollen, but dogs can bloat or torsion without visible swelling. GDV is a dire emergency condition. If you suspect a dog is bloating, you should not wait to see if he improves. A dog with GDV requires immediate veterinary care. The dog's survival usually depends on whether the owner can get him to the vet in time. It is a good idea for a standard poodle owner to know the route to the nearest 24-hour emergency clinic, so time is not wasted looking for directions.

Longevity and causes of death

Standard poodles in UK, Denmark and USA/Canada surveys had a median lifespan of 11.5 to 12 years. In a UK survey, the most common causes of death were cancer (30%), old age (18%), GDV (bloat/torsion, 6%), and cardiac disease (5%).

Miniature and toy poodles in UK surveys had median lifespans of 14 to 14.5 years. In miniature poodles, the leading cause of death was old age (39%). In toy poodles, the leading causes of death were old age (25%) and kidney failure (20%).

Some toy poodles can live up to 20 years, if they have a healthy life and are not overweight.

Common illnesses

- Addison's disease (hypoadrenocorticism)
- Cataracts
- Congenital heart disease
- Chronic active hepatitis
- Cushing's syndrome (hyperadrenocorticism)
- Distichiasis
- Entropion
- Epilepsy
- Gastric dilatation volvulus (Standard)
- Gastric torsion
- Glaucoma
- Intervertebral disc degeneration
- Lacrimal duct atresia
- Legg–Calvé–Perthes syndrome
- Progressive retinal atrophy
- Patellar luxation (Toy and Miniature)
- Trichiasis
- Urolithiasis.
- Hip dysplasia (Standard)
- Hypothyroidism
- Mitral valve disease
- Osteosarcoma
- Patent ductus arteriosus
- Sebaceous adenitis
- Von Willebrand disease

Poodle mixes

Poodles are crossed with other breeds for various reasons, and the resulting puppies (called designer dogs) are described by whimsical portmanteau words, such as cockapoo or spoodle (Cocker Spaniel cross), goldendoodle, labradoodle (Labrador cross), pekepoos (Pekingese cross), and many others.

A cross between a shedding breed and a poodle (which doesn't shed much) does not reliably produce a non-shedding dog. Traits of puppies from crossbreedings are not as predictable as those from purebred poodle breedings, and the crosses may shed or have unexpected or undesirable qualities from the parent breeds.

Poodle crossbreds (also called *hybrids*) are not recognized by any major breed registry, as crossbreeds are not one breed of dog, but two. If both parents are registered purebreds but of different breeds, it is still not possible to register a puppy as two different breeds. Some minor registries and Internet registry businesses will register dogs as any breed the owner chooses with minimal or no documentation; some even allow the breeder or owner to make up a new "breed name" (portmanteau word).

Hypoallergenic qualities

Poodles are often cited as a hypoallergenic dog breed. The poodle's individual hair follicles have an active growth period that is longer than that of many other breeds of dogs; combined with the tightly curled coat, which slows the loss of dander and dead hair by trapping it in the curls, an individual poodle may release less dander and hair into the environment. In addition, most poodles are frequently brushed and bathed to keep them looking their best; this not only removes hair and dander but also controls the other potent allergen, saliva.

Although hair, dander, and saliva can be minimized, they are still present and can stick to "clothes and the carpets and furnishings in your home"; inhaling them, or being licked by the dog, can trigger a reaction in a sensitive person. A vacuum cleaner with a HEPA filter can help clear dander floating in the air.

The word hypoallergenic, when referring to a dog, is also a misconception; all dogs shed. Poodles shed hair in minimal amounts, and also release dander, but are not as likely to trigger allergies as much as many other breeds.

Famous poodles

- Aero, Mao Asada's pet.
- Aida, pet of ice hockey player Žigmund Pálffy.
- Algonquin from *Elvira, Mistress of the Dark.*
- Atman and Butz, Schopenhauer's pets.
- Basket, Basket II, and Basket III, successive pets of Gertrude Stein and Alice B. Toklas.
- Bela, "Weird Al" Yankovic's poodle who sat on his head for the cover of his 2003 album Poodle Hat.
- Maui and Blondie, Ashley Tisdale's toy poodle and Maltipoo
- Shadow, Vanessa Hudgens' toy poodle
- Boy, pet of Prince Rupert of the Rhine (1619-1682) and killed at the Battle of Marston Moor.
- Charley, pet of Nobel Prize-winning author John Steinbeck, a black (referred to as "blue" in the book) standard poodle played Charley in the TV miniseries "Travels with Charley: In Search of America," based on Steinbeck's 1961 book of the same name.
- Cleo, from *Clifford the Big Red Dog.*
- Derek, pet of Patrick Swayze
- Diswilliam and others, pets of Mary Tyler Moore
- Dusty Springfield, Joss Stone's pet.
- Fluffles from A Matter of Loaf and Death
- Georgette from Disney's "Oliver & Company."
- Gigi and Cash, pets of Christian Serratos.
- Jane Seymour third wife of Henry VIII had a pet white poodle, which even appears in the official portrait of Henry, Jane, and his parents, the previous King and Queen. She is said to have spent most of her time walking the poodle in the palace gardens or doing needlework.
- Josephine, prized pet of author Jacqueline Susann; subject of her first book, 1963's *Every Night, Josephine!.*
- Mephistopheles, incarnated in a poodle as described by Goethe in *Faust.*
- Mugatu, from the movie Zoolander, owned a white toy poodle.
- Puff, Suga Mama's pet poodle from *The Proud Family.*
- Poodle, a pet haruno in *Honey and Clover*
- Quiche Lorraine, Fred Schneider's surreal (dark green, strawberry blonde) pet poodle in The B-52's song "Quiche Lorraine".
- Roly, a poodle who was featured in the BBC's *EastEnders* for eight years.
- Rufus, pet of Winston Churchill
- Teddy, famous dog of radio talk show host Michael Savage.
- Vicky, pet of Richard and Pat Nixon.
- Wellington, famous macguffin from *The Curious Incident of the Dog in the Night-time,* by Mark Haddon.

- Yankee Poodle from *Captain Carrot and His Amazing Zoo Crew!*.
- Itchy and Scratchy, Chris Packham's poodles, see
- Bunyip, resident pooch in Australian TV soap 'The Secret Life of Us'

Notes

note 1. fur is defined by the Oxford English Dictionary as "the short, soft hair of certain animals" whereas hair is defined as "any of the fine thread-like strands growing from the skin of mammals and other animals, or from the epidermis of a plant."

External links

- Dog Breed Profile - Poodle [2]

Pug

The **pug** is a "toy" (very small) breed of dog with a wrinkly, short-muzzled face, and curled tail. Pug puppies are often called **puglets**. The breed has a fine, glossy coat that comes in a variety of colors, and a compact square body with well-developed muscle. They have been described as *multum in parvo* ("much in little"), referring to the pug's personality and small size. Known in ancient China as *lo-sze*, they may have been responsible for both the modern Pekinese and King Charles spaniel. They have a Chinese origins, but were popularised in Western Europe by the House of Orange of the Netherlands and the House of Stuart of England, Ireland and Scotland.

They can suffer from a variety of health issues, including overheating, obesity, pharyngeal reflex and two fatal conditions which are necrotizing meningoencephalitis and hemivertebrae. In addition, care must be taken by their owner to clean the folds of skin on their face.

Description

The breed is often summarized as *multum in parvo* ("much in little"), describing the pug's remarkable personality despite its small size.While the pugs appearing in eighteenth century prints tended to be long and lean, modern breed preferences are for a square, cobby body, a compact form, a deep chest, and well-developed muscle. Pugs have two distinct shapes for their ears, "rose" and "button". "Rose" ears are smaller than the standard style "button" and are folded with the front edge against the side of the head. Breeding preference goes to "button" style pugs. The legs are very strong, straight, of moderate length, and are set well under. The shoulders are moderately laid back. The pasterns are strong, neither steep nor down. The feet are neither so long as the foot of the hare, nor so round as that of the cat; well split-up toes, and the nails black. The lower teeth normally protrude further than their upper, meeting in an under-bite.

Coat and color

Their fine, glossy coats can be fawn, apricot, silver or black. There is also the rarer white pug which gets its coat via breeding or albinism. A silver coat is characterized by a very light coloured coat, absent of black guard hairs. A silver pug typically has a very dark head, with no clear delineation at the mask, and dark forelegs. The markings are clearly defined. The trace is a black line extending from the occiput to the tail. The tail normally curls tightly over the hip.

Different coat types shed to varying degrees, but they all shed quite a bit year round. Fawns, which have both an undercoat and an overcoat, are the most notorious for shedding. Regular coat grooming can keep the shedding down.

Temperament

Strong willed but rarely aggressive, the pug is suitable for families with children. The majority of the breed is very fond of children and sturdy enough to properly play with them. They can be quiet and docile but also vivacious and teasing depending on their owner's mood. They can make good watchdogs, they are always alert and sometimes yappy.

History

Origins

Bred to adorn the laps of the Chinese sovereigns during the Shang dynasty (before 400 BCE), in East China, they were known as "Lo-Chiang-Sze" or "Foo" (ceramic foos, transmogrified into dragon, with their bulging eyes are similar in appearance to the pug). References to pug-like dogs have been documented as early as 551 BCE by Confucius, who described a type of "short mouthed dog". The *lo-sze* or early pug may have been the predecessor of today's modern Pekingese. The pug's popularity spread to Tibet, where they were mainly kept by Buddhist monks, and then went on to Japan, and finally Europe. The exact origins of the pug are unknown, as Emperor Qin Shi Huang, the first Emperor of China, destroyed all records, scrolls and art related to the pug at some point during his reign which lasted between 221 and 210 BCE.

Chinese *fu* dogs, also called lion dogs or *fo* dogs, were thought of as guardians and statues of them were placed outside temples. The faces of these statues resemble Oriental short-faced dogs, such as the Tibetan spaniel, Lhasa apso, Pekinese and the pug.

16th and 17th centuries

The breed was first imported in the late 16th and 17th centuries by merchants and crews from the Dutch East India Company. The pug later became the official dog of the House of Orange. In 1572, a pug named Pompey saved the Prince of Orange's life by barking at an assassin. A pug also traveled with William III and Mary II when they left the Netherlands to ascend to the throne of England in 1688. During this period the pug may have been bred with the old type King Charles Spaniel, but in any event the modern English Toy/King Charles Spaniel emerged with pug characteristics.

This century also saw the breed's popularity on the rise in other European countries. They were painted by Goya in Spain and in Italy they were dressed in matching jackets and pantaloons whilst sat up front next to the coachmen of the rich. They were used by the military to track animals and people, and were also employed as guard dogs.

18th and 19th centuries

The popularity of the pug continued to spread in France during the eighteenth century. Before her marriage to Napoleon Bonaparte, Joséphine had her pug, Fortune, carry concealed messages to her family while she was confined at Les Carmes prison. The pet was the only recipient of visiting rights. The pug was also well known in Italy. In 1789, a Mrs. Piozzi wrote in her journal, "The little pug dog or Dutch mastiff has quitted London for Padua, I perceive. Every carriage I meet here has a pug in it."

The English painter William Hogarth owned a series of pugs, to which he was devoted. In 1745 he painted his self-portrait together with that of his pug, Trump, now in the Tate Gallery, London.

In nineteenth century England, the breed flourished under the patronage of the monarch Queen Victoria. Her many pugs, which she bred herself, included Olga, Pedro, Minka, Fatima and Venus. Her involvement with the dogs in general helped to establish the Kennel Club, which was formed in 1873. Victoria favoured apricot and fawn colors, whereas the aristocrat Lady Brassey is credited with making black pugs fashionable after she brought some back from China in 1886.

In paintings and engravings of the 18th and 19th centuries, they usually appeared with longer legs and noses, and with cropped ears. The modern pug's appearance probably appeared after 1860 when a new wave of pugs were imported directly from China. These pugs had shorter legs and the modern style pug nose. Ear cropping was outlawed in 1895.

The pug arrived in the United States during the nineteenth century (the American Kennel Club recognized the breed in 1885) and was soon making its way into the family home and show ring. In 1981 the pug *Dhandys Favorite Woodchuck* won the Westminster Kennel Club show in the United States, the only pug to have won since the show began in 1877. The World Champion (Best in Show or BIS) at the 2004 World Dog Show held in Rio de Janeiro, Brazil was a pug, *Double D Cinoblu's Masterpiece*. The Pug Dog Club of America was founded in 1931 and recognized by the AKC that same year.

Health problems

Since pugs lack longer snouts and prominent skeletal brow ridges, they are susceptible to eye injuries such as puncture wounds and scratched corneas and painful entropion. They also have compact breathing passageways, leaving many unable to breathe properly or efficiently or their ability to regulate their temperature through evaporation from the tongue. A pug's normal body temperature is between and . If the temperature rises to they are no longer able to cope with cooling themselves and their oxygen demand is greatly increased, and requires cooling down immediately. Should the temperature reach , the internal organs begin to break down at a cellular level which can lead to severe long term health issues or even death.

Pugs living a mostly sedentary life can be prone to obesity, though this is avoidable with regular exercise and a healthy diet.

An investigative documentary carried out by the BBC found significant inbreeding between pedigree dogs, with a study by Imperial College, London, showing that the 10,000 pugs in the UK are so inbred that their gene pool is the equivalent of only 50 individuals

Serious issues

Pugs can suffer from necrotizing meningoencephalitis (NME), also known as pug dog encephalitis (PDE), an inflammation of the brain and meninges, that also occurs in other small-breed dogs, such as the Maltese and Chihuahua. There is no known cause or cure for NME, although it is believed to be an inherited disease. All dogs usually die or are euthanised within a few months after the onset of clinical signs, which usually occurs anywhere from 6 months to 7 years of age.

This breed, along with other brachycephalic dogs (e.g., boxers, bulldogs), are also prone to hemivertebrae. The screwtail is an example of a hemivertebrae, but when it occurs in other areas of the spine it can be devastating, causing such severe paralysis that euthanasia is a serious recommendation. The condition occurs when two parts of the spinal vertebrae do not fuse properly whilst a young pug is still growing, resulting in pressure being placed on the spine.

Common conditions

As they have many wrinkles in their faces, owners normally take special care to clean inside the creases, as irritation and infection can result from improper care. Hip dysplasia is a major problem for the breed, with 63.8% of pugs being affected according to a survey performed by the Orthopedic Foundation for Animals, and they were ranked second worst affected by the condition out of 157 breeds tested.

The pug, like other short-snouted breeds, has an elongated palate. When excited, they are prone to "reverse sneezing," where the dog will quickly, and seemingly laboriously, gasp and snort. The veterinary name for this is Pharyngeal Gag Reflex. This is caused by fluid or debris getting caught under the palate and irritating the throat or limiting breathing. "Reverse sneezing" episodes are usually not harmful to the pug and resolve themselves. Massaging the dog's throat or covering its nose in order to make it breathe through its mouth can often shorten episodes.

Pugs are one of several breeds that are more susceptible to Demodectic mange, also known as Demodex. This condition is caused by a weakened immune system, and it is a minor problem for many young pugs. This causes them to catch diseases much more easily than regular dogs do. It is easily treatable although some are especially susceptible and will present with a systemic form of the condition. This vulnerability is thought to be genetic, and breeders avoid breeding dogs who have had this condition. Inbreeding is also a known cause for these problems.

Media and culture

Pugs have been featured in television and film, including Frank the Pug in the film *Men in Black*, its sequel and the follow-up animated series. Other films featuring the breed include *The Adventures of Milo and Otis*, Disney's *Pocahontas*, *12 Rounds*, *Marie Antoinette*. and Dune. On television, they have appeared in shows such as *The King of Queens*, *Spin City*, *Legend of the Dragon*, *The West Wing* and *Eastenders*.

Pugs have also appeared in a variety of fictional print media, including the hypnotic Petula in the "Molly Moon" series, Lady Bertram's pug in *Mansfield Park* and in the book *Pugs: God's Little Weirdos*, a spin off from the *Sheldon* web comic. They also featured in Nintendogs for the Nintendo DS handheld video game console and a "Perky Pug" pet can be accessed in Blizzard Entertainment's *World of Warcraft*. Cheeka is a famous pug who appeared in the "You & I" advertising campaign of Hutch's cellular service in India.

Celebrity pug owners include financial talk show host and best selling author Dave Ramsey, comedienne Maria Bamford, broadcaster Jonathan Ross, actress Jessica Alba, actor Hugh Laurie, fashion designer Valentino Garavani, footballer Zlatan Ibrahimovic, actor Gerard Butler, actress Jenna Elfman and musician Rob Zombie.

In a 23 May 2007, web issue of *The Onion*, the breed was lampooned in a fake news article titled "Dog Breeders Issue Massive Recall of '07 Pugs". The piece satirized pugs and their breeders by writing of the dog and its characteristics as a faulty product, "evidenced" by a fictional quote from the American Pug Breeders Association director: "While pug owners are accustomed to dog malfunction, the latest animals are prone to more problems than just the usual joint failures, overheating, seizures, chronic respiratory defects, and inability to breed without assistance. The latest model Pug is simply not in any way a viable dog."

See also

- Companion dog
- Companion Group
- *Foo* dogs (or *fu* dogs), dog breeds originating in China that resemble Chinese guardian lions and hence are also called "lion dogs"
- Lap dog
- Toy Group
- Puggle
- Ori-Pei

External links

- Precious Little Pugs [1] - slideshow by *Life magazine*

National breed clubs

- Pug Dog Club of America [2]
- UK Pug Dog Club [3]
- Pug Club of Canada [4]
- Malta Pug Dog Club [5]

Shih Tzu

The **Shih Tzu** (, from Mandarin) is a breed of small but very ancient dog type, with long silky fur. The breed originated in China. The name is both singular and plural.

Names and etymology

Shih Tzu (), is the Chinese name rendered according to the Wade-Giles system of romanization in use when the breed was first introduced in America; the Chinese pronunciation is approximately . The name translates as Lion Dog, so named because the dog was bred to resemble "the lion as depicted in traditional oriental art," such as the Chinese guardian lions. The Shih Tzu is also often known as the "Xi Shi quan" (西施犬), based on the name of Xi Shi, regarded as the most beautiful woman of ancient China, and, less often, the Chrysanthemum Dog, a nickname coined in England in the 1930s. The dog may also be called the Tibetan Lion Dog, but whether or not the breed should be referred to as a Tibetan or Chinese breed is a source of argument, the absolute answer to which "may never be known".

Appearance

A small dog with a short muzzle and large deep dark eyes, with a soft long, double coat, the Shih Tzu stands no more than 26.7 cm (10 1/2 in.) at the withers and with an ideal weight of 4.5 to 7.3 kg (10 to 16 lbs). Drop ears are covered with long fur, and the heavily furred tail is carried curled over the back. The coat may be of any color, although a blaze of white on the forehead and tail-tip is frequently seen. The Shih Tzu is slightly longer than tall, and dogs ideally should carry themselves "with distinctly arrogant carriage." A very noticeable feature is the underbite, which is required in the breed standard.

The traditional long silky glossy coat that reaches the floor requires daily brushing to avoid tangles. Often the coat is clipped short to simplify care, in a "puppy clip". For conformation showing, the coat must be left in its natural state, although trimming for neatness around the feet and anus is allowed. Because Shih Tzu noses are small and flat, owners often wipe the dog's face with a damp paper towel to remove food remnants after the dog has eaten a meal. Shih Tzu may be trained to drink out of a water bottle. The water bottle keeps the face clean and dry preventing red yeast from growing on the Shih Tzu beard and moustache. Owners often tie strands of hair from the Shih Tzu's head into a pony tail that sticks up.

History

Recent DNA analysis confirms that the ancestors of today's Shih Tzu breed are among the most ancient of dog breeds. Ludvic von Schulmuth studied the skeletal remains of dogs found in human settlements as long as ten thousand years ago. Von Schulmuth created a genealogical tree of Tibetan dogs that shows the "Gobi Desert Kitchen Midden Dog", a scavenger, evolved into the "Small Soft-Coated Drop-Eared Hunting Dog who would fight lions in packs " which evolved into the Tibetan Spaniel, Pekingese, and Japanese Chin. Another branch coming down from the "Kitchen Midden Dog" gave rise to the Papillon and Long-haired Chihuahua and yet another "Kitchen Midden Dog" branch to the Pug and Shih Tzu. The Shih Tzu was almost completely wiped out during the Chinese Revolution. Seven males and seven females were saved, and today, all shih tzus can be traced back to one of these dogs.

There are various theories of the origins of today's breed. Theories relate that it stemmed from a cross between Pekingese and a Tibetan dog called the Lhasa Apso; that the Chinese court received a pair as a gift during the Tang Dynasty (618 – 907 AD); and that they were introduced from Tibet to China in the mid-18th century (Qing Dynasty. Dogs during that time were selectively bred and seen in Chinese paintings. The first dogs of the breed were imported into Europe (England and Norway) in 1930, and were classified by the Kennel Club as "Apsos". The first European standard for the breed was written in England in 1935 by the Shih Tzu Club, and the dogs were recatagorised as Shih Tzu. The breed spread throughout Europe, and was brought to the United States after World War II, when returning members of the US military brought back dogs from Europe. The Shih Tzu was recognised by the American Kennel Club in 1969 in the Toy Group. The breed is now recognised by all of the major kennel clubs in the English-speaking world. It is also recognised by the Fédération Cynologique Internationale for international competition in Companion and Toy Dog Group, Section 5, Tibetan breeds.

Health

A number of health issues, some of them hereditary, have been found in individual Shih Tzu, and are listed below. There is no data on the percentage of dogs with these ailments.

Morbidity

Some health issues in the breed are portosystemic shunt of the liver and hip dysplasia in standard sizes.

Breathing problems

Shih Tzu are brachycephalic (short-muzzled) dogs and are very sensitive to high temperatures. Many airlines that ship dogs will not accept them for shipment when temperatures at any point on the planned itinerary exceeds 75 °F (24 °C).

Mortality

The life span of a Shih Tzu is 12-16 years although some variation from this range is possible.

Temperament

The Shih Tzu is a friendly lap dog that at one time was bred to be a companion dog for Chinese royalty. Some say living in the imperial palace gave the Shih Tzu an arrogant quality, although they also display qualities of devotion and adaptability. They are not afraid to stand up for themselves. They tend to be sweet, playful, and trusting as well. They should be introduced to young children at a young age. It ranks 70th in Stanley Coren's The Intelligence of Dogs, considered one of the lowest degree of working/obedience intelligence (trainability).

Coat Colors

The Shih Tzu comes in a range of colors that include various shades of gold and white and red and white. Other colors include black mask gold, solid red, black and white, solid black, solid liver, liver and white, blue and white, brindle and white and silver and white. Though not as common there are also solid blue Shih Tzu. An interesting point (and often a point of confusion) is that while the coat color of those with black pigmented skin (nose, lips, pads, also referred to as "leather") is determined by the color of the coat itself; the coat color on dogs with either liver or blue pigment is categorized by the colour of the pigment. Thus a parti colored (white and another shade) Shih Tzu with blue pigment is a "blue and white" regardless of the tint of the hair which might very well appear similar to a gold and white or other colors. The same principle applies to solid blue, liver and liver and white.

Size and Description misunderstanding

Some refer to the Shih Tzu as teacup, toy, toi, pint-size, pocket, imperial, IMP, Chinese imperial dog, CID, miniature or standard but all these references are considered inappropriate and are categorically rejected by the American Shih Tzu Club, Inc. as the National Breed Club maintains there is but one "Shih Tzu" and the ideal weight is 9-16 lbs. (That does not negate the fact that size may vary and those smaller than what is defined as the ideal are not uncommon in litters produced by sires and dams that fall within the ideal weight range.) The use of such descriptive labels is generally regarded as a marketing ploy, as is pitching Shih Tzu to be of "rare color." and great pets

Hypoallergenic coats

The Shih Tzu is one of many dog breeds with a hypoallergenic coat. This makes the Shih Tzu a perfect dog for owners with allergies to pet dander.

Variations

Size issues

There is no such thing as a "teacup" Shih Tzu nor a "toy sized" Shih Tzu. Imperial Shih Tzu is a term used by breeders to sell Shih Tzu that are below healthy standard size. These tiny dogs, often less than 50% of the recommended minimum size, are prone to serious health problems and may not live a full life span. Many are created by breeding the runt of one litter with the runt of another litter.

Kennel club differences

There is a difference between the American Kennel Club and the Kennel Club (UK) Shih Tzu:

The AKC (american kennel club) Shih Tzu

- Their legs are high and the front legs face forward.
- The chest is small.
- The head is more or less square-ish and is set on a very long and slender neck
- The eyes are large and do not face the front completely.
- The shoulders of the American type of Shih Tzu are frontal.

Crosses with other breeds

A crossbreed or dog hybrid is a dog with two purebred parents of different breeds. Dogs traditionally were crossed in this manner in hopes of creating a puppy with desirable qualities from each parent, but when two different breeds are mixed, there is no way to know which traits will be inherited from each parent. For pet dogs such as the Shih Tzu, crosses are done to enhance the marketability of puppies, resulting in "Designer" dogs with portmanteau names such as Shih-poo (a Shih Tzu crossbred with a toy Poodle) and ShiChi (cross between Shih-Tzu and Chihuahua). It is fashionable to merchandise crossbreed and mixed breed dogs with the word *hybrid*, which implies two different species, but all Shih Tzu and Shih Tzu crosses are of the sub-species *Canis lupus familiaris*. As with all dogs born of parents who are not the same breed, "designer" dogs are not purebreds, and therefore are not eligible for purebred registries such as the American Kennel Club.

External links

- AKC Shih Tzu Video [1]

Australian Silky Terrier

The **Australian Silky Terrier** is a small breed of dog of the terrier dog type. The breed was developed in Australia, although the ancestral types and breeds were from Great Britain. It is closely related to the Australian Terrier and the Yorkshire Terrier. The breed is called the *Silky Terrier* in North America, but is called the *Australian Silky Terrier* in its country of origin and in the rest of the world.

Appearance

The Australian Silky Terrier is a small and compact short legged terrier, 23 to 26 cms (9 to 10 ins) at the withers, alert and active. The long silky blue and tan coat is an identifying feature, hanging straight and parted along the back, and described as "flat, fine and glossy". All proportions and aspects of the body and head as well as desirable shades of blue and tan and placement of markings are extensively described in the breed standard.

The Silky Terrier should be slightly longer than tall (about one fifth longer that the height at withers). This is a dog that was historically used for hunting and killing rodents, so its body should have enough substance to fit this role. The coat requires quite a lot of regular grooming and shampooing to retain its silkiness.

Silky terrier has strong and wedge-shaped head. The eyes are small and almond shaped. According to the standards, light-colored eyes are considered a fault. The ears are small and carried erect. Silky terrier has a high-set tail and small, almost catlike, feet. The coat should be long, but not so long to approach floor length. The hair on the face and ears is normally cut.

History

The ancestors of the Australian Silky Terrier include the Yorkshire Terrier (originally from Scotland before being considered to be from England) and the Australian Terrier,(which descends from the rough coated type terriers brought from Great Britain to Australia in the early 1800s) few records to indicate whether early dogs were just Australian Terriers born with silky fur, or whether there was an attempt to create a separate breed. According to the American Kennel Club, the breed began at the end of the 1800s when Yorkshire Terriers were crossed with the Australian Terriers. At first the breed was known as the Sydney Silky, as it was found primarily in the city of Sydney, Australia. Although most other Australian breeds were working dogs, the Silky Terrier was bred primarily to be an urban pet and companion, although it is also known for killing snakes in Australia.

Up until 1929 the Australian Terrier, the Australian Silky Terrier, and the Yorkshire Terrier were not clearly defined. Dogs of three different breeds might be born in the same litter, to be separated by appearance into the different types once they were grown. After 1932 in Australia, further crossbreeding was discouraged, and in 1955 the breed's name officially became the Australian Silky Terrier. The breed was recognised by the Australian National Kennel Council in 1958 in the Toy Group.

During and after World War II American servicemen that had been stationed in Australia brought back to the United States a few Silky Terriers. Newspaper photographs of the breed in 1954 caused an upsurge of popularity and hundreds of Silkies were imported from Australia to the United States. The American Kennel Club recognised the breed as the Silky Terrier in 1959, as did the United Kennel Club (US) in 1965; it is also recognised as the Silky Terrier by the Canadian Kennel Club. The breed is recognised by all the major kennel clubs in the English speaking world, and internationally by the Fédération Cynologique Internationale as breed number 236. It may also be recognised by various minor kennel clubs and internet breed registry businesses.

Breed Groups

The Australian Silky Terrier is a terrier, but is usually placed in the Toy Group rather than the Terrier Group due to its small size. As breed groupings are done mostly to organise groups of breeds for dog shows, it is safer for the little dogs to be with others their own size, rather than with larger dogs. The Fédération Cynologique Internationale has a special Section of the Terrier Group that includes only the smallest dogs, while other kennel clubs place the breed in the Toy Group, but universally everyone agrees that the breed's type is Terrier.

Health

The Silky is prone to several disorders including luxating patella, tracheal collapse, and epilepsy. These dogs are very sensitive to voice tone. A loud deep tone will frighten them, and a high squeaky shriek will make them freeze. The Silky Terrier enjoys back scratches and can be rendered immobile by scratching the hindquarters.

Temperament

The breed standard describe the ideal Australian Silky Terrier temperament as keenly alert and active. They love to be given chances to run and play, but must have a tightly fenced yard. They also enjoy brisk walks and playing ball. The Silky is able to do well in an apartment, although they are also an active indoor breed. It is important they are kept busy and social to discourage boredom. They are also rodent hunters. They have a lifespan of 12 to14 years.

Care

The Silky Terrier's coat is highly susceptible to tangles and matting. They require daily brushing and combing. This breed requires a deep commitment from their owners. To keep the coat lustrous regular shampooing is necessary. Using an Avocado and Oatmeal Shampoo will help alleviate the itchy, dry skin of this breed. For this particular breed, you should take your pet to the groomers every 3 weeks and have his teeth brushed while there. Terriers are known to have teeth and gum problems. As well you should keep your terrier on a harness leash not a collar due to the terriers weak and collapsible trachea or windpipe.

See also

- Yorkshire Terrier
- Australian Terrier

References

Additional reading

- *History, Origins and Development of the Australian Silky Terrier* George Holmes. One of several essays appearing in *Australian Made: Australian Breeds Feature*, privately published, mid-1990.

External links

- Silky Terrier Club Of America [1]

Toy Fox Terrier

The **Toy Fox Terrier** is a small terrier breed of dog, directly descended from the larger Fox Terrier but considered a separate breed.

Description

Appearance

Toy Fox Terriers are small dogs with a muscular and athletic appearance. Notable characteristic traits include a short glossy and predominantly white coat, coupled with a predominantly solid head, and a short, high-set tail. The breed has been deemed elegant and graceful with V-shaped ears and large eyes. The tail can be short and straight, and breeders often shorten the tail a few days after birth by clipping it about three-fifth of the way from the tip (at the third or fourth joint). The coat is short, fine, and glossy in white with black, with areas of tan on the face; there are two other variants, one with 'chocolate' replacing the black in areas (the UKC does not allow this variant to be shown), and another which is all white and tan with no black at all. These variants are often known as 'Tri-Color', 'Chocolate', and 'Tan and White', respectively. The height ranges from 8.5–11.5 inches at the shoulder (21.5–29.2 cm) and weight from 3.5-9 pounds. They are in many ways similar to the Miniature Fox Terrier.

Temperament

Toy Fox Terriers, like many active and intelligent breeds, can learn to respond to a number of words. Toy Fox Terriers were used commonly in circus shows by clowns, and they are said to make great companions for owners with a good sense of humor. As a terrier breed, they are often very active, though perhaps not as active as the Jack Russell Terrier, and are said to be well suited for older owners. They are quite trainable and often cited as making wonderful companions for people with disabilities. They are also very lovable and loyal to their owners. In addition, dogs of this breed tend not to bark very much if they are trained well.

About

Toy Fox Terriers adapt well to apartment life. They are active indoors and will do without a yard, as they can usually take care of their own exercise needs. They often have trouble tolerating cold weather without careful acclimation. Their life expectancy is about fifteen years (since the breed has only been officially recognized by groups like the UKC and the AKC since 2000, there is little official documentation). Toy Fox Terriers are significantly healthful and resilient, however, as with many toy breeds, some are prone to patellar luxation (slipped stifle). Legg-Calvé-Perthes syndrome and von Willebrand's disease are uncommon. Some dogs are allergic to beet pulp, corn, and wheat. The Toy

Fox Terrier is easy to groom, although grooming is generally seen as unneeded due to how short the hairs are (under a centimetre in length most of the time). Sometimes, it is necessary to comb and brush the coat. The hairs shed very frequently.

History

Some Toy Fox Terrier breeders can trace their dogs' lineage back to a Smooth Fox Terrier called "Foiler", the first fox terrier registered by the Kennel Club in Britain, circa 1875-76. It is believed that careful breeding from smaller Smooth Fox Terriers without crosses to other toy breeds such as Manchester Terrier and Chihuahua resulted in the Toy Fox Terrier of today.

Toy Fox Terriers were recognized by the United Kennel Club (UKC) in 1936 and placed in the Terrier Group, and by the American Kennel Club (AKC) in July 2000 (Toy Group).

See also

- Fox Terrier, for additional details on history, genetics, coat color, etc.
- Rare breeds

References

- Davidson, John F., *The Toy Fox Terrier - Wired for Action* (a 2006 revision of *The Toy Fox Terrier*)
- Hopkins, Eliza and Flamholtz, Cathy *The Toy Fox Terrier*
- Bielsky-Braham, Tanya, *Send in the Clowns*. AKC Gazette, December, 2002

Yorkshire Terrier

The **Yorkshire terrier** is a small dog breed of Terrier type, developed in the 1800s in the historical area of Yorkshire in England. The defining features of the breed are its small size, less than 7 pounds, and its silky blue and tan coat. The breed is nicknamed *Yorkie* and is placed in the Toy Terrier section of the Terrier Group by the Fédération Cynologique Internationale and in the Toy Group or Companion Group by other kennel clubs, although all agree that the breed is a terrier. A winning showdog and a popular companion dog, the Yorkshire terrier has also been part of the development of other breeds, such as the Australian Silky Terrier.

Coat

For adult Yorkshire terriers, the importance is placed on its coat colour, its quality, and its texture. The hair must be glossy, fine, straight, and silky. Traditionally the coat is grown-out long and is parted down the middle of the back, but "must never impede movement."

Yorkies have very soft coats. Yorkies have two types of coats; a silky or a soft. The silky coats are the coats of the show dogs. The soft coats are short and do not need to be brushed very often.

From the back of the neck to the base of the tail, the coat should be a dark gray to a steel-blue, and the hair on the tail should be a darker blue. On the head, high chest, and legs, the hair should be a bright, rich tan, darker at the roots than in the middle, that shades into a lighter tan at the tips. Also, in adult dogs, there should be no dark hairs intermingled with any of the tan coloured fur.

Adult Yorkshire terriers that have other coat colours than the above, or that have wooly or extra fine coats, are still considered to be Yorkshire terriers, and will be just as good of a companion as a dog with the correct coat. The only difference is that atypical Yorkshire terriers should not be bred. In addition, care may be more difficult for "wooley" or "cottony" textured coats, or coats that are overly fine. One of the reasons given for not breeding "off-coloured" Yorkies is that the colour could be linked to a genetic defect that may affect the dog's health.

Puppy coats

A newborn Yorkie puppy is born black with tan points on the muzzle, above the eyes, around the legs and feet and toes, the inside of the ears, and the underside of the tail.. Occasionally Yorkies are born with a white "star" on the chest or on one or more toes. These markings fade with age, and are usually gone within a few months. A white "star" on the chest is generally an indication that the puppy will be a good coat grower in quantity, but not necessarily quality.

It may take up to three years or more for the coat to reach its final colour. P. H. Coombs, writing in 1891, complained about show wins awarded to puppies, when the dog's coat does not fully come in until three or four years old, "and the honour of winning such a prize (for a puppy) can therefore be of but little practical benefit to the owner" since the adult dog's colour cannot be exactly predicted.

Hypoallergenic coats

The typical fine, straight, and silky Yorkshire terrier coat has also been listed by many popular dog information websites as being hypoallergenic. In comparison with many other breeds, Yorkies do not shed to the same degree, only losing small amounts when bathed or brushed. All dogs shed, and it is the dog's dander and saliva that trigger most allergic reactions. Allergists do recognise that at times a particular allergy patient will be able to tolerate a particular dog, but they agree that "the luck of the few with their pets cannot be stretched to fit all allergic people and entire breeds of dogs." The Yorkshire terrier coat is said to fall out only when brushed or broken, or just said to not shed. Although neither of those statements agree with what biologists, veterinarians, and allergists know about dog fur, allergists "think there really are differences in protein production between dogs that may help one patient and not another", meaning that some allergic people may not have allergic reactions to a specific dog, like the Yorkie.

Coat care

If the coat is the correct silky texture, maintenance for it is relatively easy, requiring a daily brushing and a bath every month. Owners may trim the fur short for easier care. For shows, the coat is left long, and may be trimmed to floor length to give ease of movement and a neater appearance. Hair on the feet and the tips of ears can also be trimmed.

The traditional long coat is extremely high maintenance. To prevent breakage, the coat may be wrapped in rice paper, tissue paper, or plastic, after a light oiling with a coat oil. The oil has to be washed out once a month and the wraps must be fixed periodically during the week to prevent them from sliding down and breaking the hair. Elaborate care of the beautiful coat dates from the earliest days of the breed. In 1878, John Walsh described similar preparations: the coat is "well greased" with coconut oil, the dog is bathed weekly, and the dog's feet are "carefully kept in stockings."

Other colors

The Yorkshire terrier is a tan dog with a blue saddle. Parti colours exist, although they are not correct for the breed standard. The parti colour coat Is white with black/blue and tan. It's very rare to get a a parti colour yorkie, and if they are found they tend to be very expensive. The breed is defined by its colour, and colours promoted as "rare" may indicate health problems or cross-breeding with other breeds of other colours. The AKC registration form for Yorkshire terriers allows for four choices: blue and tan, blue and gold, black and tan, black and gold. Colour alone will not affect whether or not a dog is a good companion and pet. Even though off-coloured Yorkshire terriers are advertised at premium prices, being of an unusual or untypical colour is neither new, desirable, nor exotic.

Until recently, mismarked Yorkshire terriers could be crossed with Biewer terriers, a new breed originated in Germany from parti coloured Yorkshire terriers. Although the American Kennel Club will not deny registration of a Yorkshire terrier on colour alone, the Yorkshire terrier Club of America has a directive that "any solid colour or combination of colours other than blue and tan" for adult dogs is a disqualification, and "dogs of solid colour, unusual combination of colours, and parti-colours should be disqualified." by

Character

The ideal Yorkshire terrier character or "personality" is described with a "carriage very upright" and "conveying an important air". Though small, the Yorkshire terrier is active, loves attention and should not show the soft temperament seen in lapdogs.

Boldness

The Yorkshire terrier breed is bold and active.They are brave for such a small breed. They are, however, also quite loyal and affectionate. Yorkshire terrier puppies are especially loving and cuddly with their owners in their first 2-3 years.

History

The Yorkshire terrier originated in Yorkshire (and the adjoining Lancashire), a rugged region in northern England. In the mid-nineteenth century, workers from Scotland came to Yorkshire in search of work and brought with them several different varieties of small terriers. Breeding of the Yorkshire terrier was "principally accomplished by the people--mostly operatives in cotton and woolen mills--in the counties of Yorkshire and Lancashire." Details are scarce. Mrs. A. Foster is quoted as saying in 1886, "If we consider that the mill operatives who originated the breed...were nearly all ignorant men, unaccustomed to imparting information for public use, we may see some reason why reliable facts have not been easily attained."

What is known is that the breed sprang from three different dogs, a male named Old Crab and a female named Kitty, and another female whose name is not known. The Paisley Terrier, a smaller version of the Skye Terrier that was bred for a beautiful long silky coat, also figured into the early dogs. Some authorities believed that the Maltese was used as well. "They were all originally bred from Scotch terriers (note: meaning dogs from Scotland, not today's Scottish Terrier) and shown as such...the name Yorkshire terrier was given to them on account of their being improved so much in Yorkshire." Yorkshire terriers were shown in a dog show category (class) at the time called "Rough and Broken-coated, Broken-haired Scotch and Yorkshire terriers". Hugh Dalziel, writing in 1878, says that "the classification of these dogs at shows and in the Kennel Club Stud Book is confusing and absurd" in lumping together these different types.

In the early days of the breed, "almost anything in the shape of a Terrier having a long coat with blue on the body and fawn or silver coloured head and legs, with tail docked and ears trimmed, was received and admired as a Yorkshire terrier". But in the late 1860s, a popular Paisley type Yorkshire terrier showdog named Huddersfield Ben, owned by a woman living in Yorkshire, Mary Ann Foster, was seen at dog shows throughout Great Britain, and defined the breed type for the Yorkshire terrier.

Huddersfield Ben

Huddersfield Ben was a famous dog. His portrait was painted by George Earl and in 1891 an authority on the breed wrote, "Huddersfield Ben was the best stud dog of his breed during his life-time, and one of the most remarkable dogs of any pet breed that ever lived; and most of the show specimens of the present day have one or more crosses of his blood in their pedigree." A show winner, Huddersfield Ben quickly became the type of dog everyone wanted, and through his puppies has defined the breed as we know it today. He is still referred to as "father of the breed".

In America

The Yorkshire terrier was introduced in the North America in 1872 and the first Yorkshire terrier was registered with the American Kennel Club (AKC) in 1878, making it one of the first twenty-five breeds to be approved for registration by the AKC. During the Victorian era, the Yorkshire terrier was a popular pet and showdog in England, and as Americans embraced Victorian customs, so too did they embrace the Yorkshire terrier. The breed's popularity dipped in the 1940s, when the percentage of small breed dogs registered fell to an all-time low of 18% of total registrations. Smoky, a Yorkshire terrier and famous war dog from World War II, is credited with beginning a renewal of interest in the breed.

Health

A number of health issues, some of them hereditary, have been found in individual Yorkshire terriers, and are listed below. There is no data on the percentage of dogs with these ailments, and it is not suggested that all Yorkshire terriers have all of these ailments, or that any particular dog has any of these ailments. Puppy buyers are advised to ask breeders if tests have been done for these diseases.

Morbidity

Health issues often seen in the Yorkshire terrier include bronchitis, lymphangiectasia, Portosystemic shunt, cataracts, and keratitis sicca. Additionally, injection reactions (inflammation or hair loss at the site of an injection) can occur. In addition they may have skin allergies.

Genetic defects

Certain genetic disorders have been found in Yorkshire terriers, including distichiasis, hydrocephalus, hypoplasia of dens, Legg–Calvé–Perthes syndrome, luxating patella, portosystemic shunt, retinal dysplasia, tracheal collapse, and bladder stones. The following are among the most common congenital defects that affect Yorkies.

- Distichiae, eyelashes arising from an abnormal spot (usually the duct of the meibomian gland at the edge of the eyelid), are often found in Yorkies. Distichiae can irritate the eye and cause tearing, squinting, inflammation, corneal abrasions or corneal ulcers, and scarring. Treatment options may include manual removal, electrolysis, or surgery.

- Hypoplasia of dens is a non-formation of the pivot point of the second cervical vertebra, which leads to spinal cord damage. Onset of the condition may occur at any age, producing signs ranging from neck pain to quadriplegia.

- Legg–Calvé–Perthes syndrome, which causes the top of the femur (thigh bone) to degenerate, occurs in Yorkies in certain lines. The condition appears to result from insufficient circulation to the area around the hip joint. As the blood supply is reduced, the bone in the head of the femur collapses and dies and the cartilage coating around it becomes cracked and deformed. Usually the disease appears when the Yorkie is young (between five and eight months of age); signs are pain, limping, or lameness. The standard treatment is surgery to remove the affected part of the bone. Following surgery, muscles hold the femur in place and fibrous tissue forms in the area of removal to prevent bone rubbing on bone. Although the affected leg will be slightly shorter than prior to surgery, the Yorkie may regain almost normal use.

- Luxating patellas (slipping kneecaps) are another common defect considered to be genetic in Yorkies, although it may also be caused by an accidental fall. Weak ligaments and tendons in the knee or malformed (too shallow) patellar grooves, allow the patella to slip out of its groove sideways. This causes the leg to 'lock up' with the foot held off the ground. A dog with this problem may experience frequent pain and lameness or may be bothered by it only on occasion. Over time, the patellar ridges can become worn down, making the groove even more shallow and causing the dog to become increasingly lame. Surgery is the main treatment option available for luxating patellas, although it is not necessary for every dog with the condition.

- Portosystemic shunt, a congenital malformation of the portal vein (which brings blood to the liver for cleansing), is also common in Yorkies. In this condition some of the dog's blood bypasses the liver and the "dirty" blood goes on to poison the heart, brain, lungs, and other organs with toxins. A Yorkie with this condition might exhibit a wide variety of symptoms, such as small stature, poor appetite, weak muscle development, decreased ability to learn, inferior coordination, occasional vomiting and diarrhea, behavioral abnormalities, seizures (especially after a meal), and blindness, which could lead to a coma and death. Often, the shunt can be treated with surgery.

- Tracheal collapse, caused by a progressive weakening of the walls of the trachea, occurs in many toy breeds, especially very tiny Yorkies. As a result of genetics, the walls of the trachea can be flaccid, a condition that becomes more severe with age. Cushing's syndrome, a disorder that causes production of excess steroid hormone by the adrenal glands, can also weaken cartilage and lead to tracheal collapse. There is a possibility that physical strain on the neck might cause or contribute to trachea collapse. Since this is usually caused by an energetic Yorkie pulling against his collar, many veterinarians recommend use of a harness for leashed walks. An occasional "goose honking" cough, especially on exertion or excitement, is usually the first sign of this condition. Over time, the cough may become almost constant in the Yorkie's later life. Breathing through the obstruction of a collapsed (or partially collapsed) trachea for many years can result in complications, including chronic lung disease. The coughing can be countered with cough suppressants and bronchodilators. If the collapse is advanced and unresponsive to medication, sometimes surgery can repair the trachea.

Hypoglycemia

Low blood sugar in puppies, or transient juvenile hypoglycemia, is caused by fasting (too much time between meals). In rare cases hypoglycemia may continue to be a problem in mature, usually very small, Yorkies. It is often seen in Yorkie puppies at 5 to 16 weeks of age. Very tiny Yorkie puppies are especially predisposed to hypoglycemia because a lack of muscle mass makes it difficult to store glucose and regulate blood sugar. Factors such as stress, fatigue, a cold environment, poor nutrition, and a change in diet or feeding schedule may bring on hypoglycemia. Low blood sugar can also be the result of a bacterial infection, parasite, or portosystemic liver shunt. Hypoglycemia causes the puppy to become drowsy, listless (glassy-eyed), shaky, uncoordinated, since the brain relies on sugar to function. During a hypoglycemic attack, the puppy usually has very pale or grey gums. The puppy also may not eat unless force-fed. Hypoglycemia and dehydration seem to go hand-in-hand, and force-feeding or injecting fluids may also be necessary. Additionally, a hypoglycemic Yorkie may have a lower than normal body temperature and, in extreme cases, may have a seizure or go into a coma. A dog showing symptoms should be given sugar in the form of corn syrup or NutriCal and be treated by a veterinarian immediately, as prolonged or recurring attacks of hypoglycemia can permanently damage the dog's brain. In severe cases it can be fatal.

Mortality

The life span of a healthy Yorkie is 12–15 years. Extremely under-sized Yorkies (3 pounds or less, and often promoted as "Teacups") generally have a shorter life span, as they are especially prone to health problems such as chronic diarrhoea and vomiting and are more easily injured. Even the normal small size of a Yorkshire terrier means that it can have a poor tolerance for anesthesia, and it is more likely to be killed or injured by falls, other dogs, and owner clumsiness.

Docking

Traditionally, the Yorkshire terrier's tail is docked to a medium length. Opposition to this practice began very early in the history of the breed; Hugh Dalziel, writing about Yorkshire terriers in 1878, declared that "There is no reason for mutilating pet dogs, and perfect ears and tails should be bred, not clipped into shape with scissors." Often, a Yorkshire terrier's dewclaws, if any, are removed in the first few days of life, another controversial practice.

Similar breeds and crosses

The Yorkshire terrier breed descends from larger but similar Scottish breeds such as the now extinct Paisley Terrier and the Skye Terrier. In its turn, other breeds have been created from the Yorkshire terrier, such as the Australian Silky Terrier and the Biewer Terrier, bred from a blue, white, and gold puppy they later named Schneeflocken von Friedheck, by Mr. and Mrs. Biewer of Germany. Demand for unusual pets has resulted in high prices being paid for Yorkshire terriers crossed with various other breeds, which are described with a portmanteau word made up of syllables (or sounds) from Yorkshire terrier and the breed name of the other parent. A list of such portmanteau-named crosses can be found on the List of dog hybrids page. It is fashionable to merchandise crossbreed and mixed breed dogs with the word *hybrid*, which implies two different animal species, but all Yorkshire terrier crossbreeds are just dogs.

Notablity

Show dogs

- In 1997, Champion Ozmilion Mystification became the first Yorkie to win Best in Show at Crufts, the world's largest annual dog show.
- Champion WA Mozart Dolce Sinfonia ("Mozart") is a show dog owned by socialite Sabrina A. Parisi. He was featured in the Krassimir Abramov music video for "Say Goodbye" and will star in the upcoming documentary *It's a Dog Life* from director Vibeke Muasya. On 11 May 2006, Mozart attended Krassimir's concert at the Kodak Theatre in Hollywood, becoming the first dog to enter the venue.

Small dogs

- Sylvia, a matchbox-size Yorkshire terrier owned by Arthur Marples of Blackburn, England, was the smallest dog in recorded history. The dog died in 1945 when she was two years old, at which point she stood 2.5 inches tall at the shoulder, measured 3.5 inches from nose tip to tail, and weighed 4 ounces.
- For 1995 through 2002 Guinness World Records listed a Yorkshire terrier named Big Boss, as the smallest dog in the world. Big Boss was listed at 11.94 cm (4.7 in) tall when his owner, Dr. Chai Khanchanakom of Thailand, registered the toy dog with Guinness.
- A Yorkie named Thumbelina, 5.5 inches tall and 8 inches long, held the Guinness World Record for smallest living dog prior to 1995.
- Tiny Pinocchio, an abnormally small Yorkshire terrier, has appeared on several television programs including *Oprah* and the *Today Show*.

War dogs

- Smoky, a war dog and hero of World War II, was owned by William Wynne of Cleveland, Ohio. Wynne adopted Smoky while he was serving with the 5th Air Force in the Pacific.

White House dogs

- Pasha, Tricia Nixon Cox's pet Yorkie, lived in the White House during the Richard Nixon presidency..

See also

- Yorkshire
- Historic counties of England
- Australian Silky Terrier
- Dog breeding
- Dog hybrid

External links

- Dog Breed Profile - Yorkshire Terrier [1]

Article Sources and Contributors

Dog breed *Source*: http://en.wikipedia.org/?oldid=374734086 *Contributors*: Falcon8765

American Kennel Club *Source*: http://en.wikipedia.org/?oldid=373448194 *Contributors*: 07bargem

Toy Group *Source*: http://en.wikipedia.org/?oldid=367706762 *Contributors*:

Affenpinscher *Source*: http://en.wikipedia.org/?oldid=371423218 *Contributors*: 1 anonymous edits

Griffon Bruxellois *Source*: http://en.wikipedia.org/?oldid=376103812 *Contributors*: Selmagriff

Cavalier King Charles Spaniel *Source*: http://en.wikipedia.org/?oldid=376672967 *Contributors*: Pilif12p

Chihuahua (dog) *Source*: http://en.wikipedia.org/?oldid=376603562 *Contributors*: 10metreh

Chinese Crested Dog *Source*: http://en.wikipedia.org/?oldid=376447760 *Contributors*: 1 anonymous edits

King Charles Spaniel *Source*: http://en.wikipedia.org/?oldid=376152341 *Contributors*: Ian Dalziel

Havanese *Source*: http://en.wikipedia.org/?oldid=372345640 *Contributors*: 1 anonymous edits

Italian Greyhound *Source*: http://en.wikipedia.org/?oldid=375989174 *Contributors*: 1 anonymous edits

Japanese Chin *Source*: http://en.wikipedia.org/?oldid=374702075 *Contributors*: Killerprey23

Maltese (dog) *Source*: http://en.wikipedia.org/?oldid=375743312 *Contributors*:

Toy Manchester Terrier *Source*: http://en.wikipedia.org/?oldid=366089956 *Contributors*: 1 anonymous edits

Miniature Pinscher *Source*: http://en.wikipedia.org/?oldid=376698575 *Contributors*: 1 anonymous edits

Papillon (dog) *Source*: http://en.wikipedia.org/?oldid=375635381 *Contributors*: Simple Bob

Pekingese *Source*: http://en.wikipedia.org/?oldid=376187095 *Contributors*: IronGargoyle

Pomeranian (dog) *Source*: http://en.wikipedia.org/?oldid=375186622 *Contributors*: Miyagawa

Poodle *Source*: http://en.wikipedia.org/?oldid=376462166 *Contributors*: Miyagawa

Pug *Source*: http://en.wikipedia.org/?oldid=376506701 *Contributors*: JForget

Shih Tzu *Source*: http://en.wikipedia.org/?oldid=375738733 *Contributors*: Active Banana

Australian Silky Terrier *Source*: http://en.wikipedia.org/?oldid=372723289 *Contributors*: Groyolo

Toy Fox Terrier *Source*: http://en.wikipedia.org/?oldid=373382943 *Contributors*: Coasterlover1994

Yorkshire Terrier *Source*: http://en.wikipedia.org/?oldid=375057227 *Contributors*: 1 anonymous edits

LaVergne, TN USA
14 December 2010
208751LV00009B/27/P

10